The Reference Shelf *(Continued)*

Volume 23

Volume 22

Volume 21

Volume 20

Volume 19

Volume 18

Volume 17

Volume 16

THE REFERENCE SHELF

Vol. 29   No. 1

AMERICAN HIGHWAYS TODAY

Edited by
POYNTZ TYLER

THE H. W. WILSON COMPANY
NEW YORK   1957

PREFACE

The wheel fathered the road. Invented about 3500 B.C.—probably by the Sumerians in what is now Iraq—it required a hard surface to support its concentrated load and so made useless the paths and trails and lanes that had served man for centuries. Mounted on an axle, the wheel revolutionized all transport, and from its inception to this day the diffusion of goods and ideas, of civilization itself, has been dependent on the ease and speed of its turning on the road.

The oldest road in Western history, called the Royal Road by the Persians, started at Susa near the Persian Gulf and stretched nearly two thousand miles to Smyrna on the far coast of Asia Minor. Beginning around 4500 B.C. as a path for animals and nomadic men, the coming of the wheel turned it into a high road of conquest for Babylonians, Assyrians, Egyptians, Hittites, and Phoenicians, for Medes, Persians, Greeks, and Romans. Over its smooth surface—packed hard in that dry and equable climate by the very wheels it served—rode Darius and Alexander the Great, Sennacherib and those Persian couriers whom "neither snow, nor rain, nor heat, nor gloom of night" could stay from the swift completion of their appointed rounds. Later, as part of the great East-West highway that reached from Spain to China, it saw Xenophon and his Ten Thousand; and still later it became part of the vast fifty-thousand-mile network of roads that knit the Roman Empire together and brought the Pax Romana to most of the known world.

More than the Pax Romana was lost to the West when those Roman roads fell to the obliterating forces of vandalism, vegetation, and neglect, for with them went all commerce, all transportation, and all interchange of knowledge and ideas. Their going helped to seal Europe into the mental and physical immobility of the early Middle Ages—the era of the horse and the donkey and the pack mule—and communications were disrupted for hundreds of years. Europe was rescued when commerce—

spurred by the Crusades and creeping into Europe through her ports—demanded the inland transportation that only roads could provide. Even then they were slow abuilding, for their construction was left to the noble and to the monk, to penitents and to convicts, and to local authorities and to local pride. None was sufficient, and even while Europe was conquering the world her roads were never adequate to support her mounting trade and prestige. Not until the coming of the railroads could she realize the vast might of her people and her resources, and the very coming of the railroads stifled her late-blooming effort for better highways. The result of this apathy and indifference and indecision is apparent in her roads today—obsolete, for the most part, by our standards—so that American roads are one of the few facets of our lives that are indubitably American. We inherited our laws from Europe, our language, our literary forms, and many of our customs, but our roads are our own. They were built from scratch by American effort with American tools to American needs—and they are the greatest system of highways in the world.

It is the story of these American roads that is told by the authors of this book. To them, and to their publishers, the editor extends sincere thanks for permission to use their work.

POYNTZ TYLER

January 1957

A NOTE TO THE READER

The highways discussed in this book halt, in most instances, at the city line. For a supplementary study of roads and streets in urban areas the reader should consult *Community Planning* by Herbert L. Marx, Jr. (Volume 28, Number 4 of The Reference Shelf).

CONTENTS

I. THE AMERICAN ROAD

THE PAST IS PROLOGUE [1]

Maybe it began as a footpath through the woods to the meeting house. A narrower path from the saw-pit entered it, and the trail which the traders took toward the notch in the hills. As a pair of ruts it led eastward to the town and the wharves and westward to the new country that was opening up. It kept forking in order to reach other towns and sometimes its course didn't seem to make much sense. The reason it climbed one hill was that long ago there had been a blockhouse on top to keep watch for Indian raids. It made one zigzag to compromise a dispute between villages and another to reach some small mills.

Wherever it ran, there was never a time when the road was not of absolute importance to the individual and to the community he lived in. The doctor came riding down it to see him into the world and the parson to see him out of it. It meant romance and longing: relatives coming home, friends arriving for a visit, the peddler bringing tinware and the news of the world, people going to see what kind of country stretched beyond the horizon. It was always pageantry: big herds of cattle and swine, emigrant wagons, stagecoaches, post riders, circus caravans, marching soldiers, horseless carriages. Crops went to market, ore and timber and cotton and wool went to the mills, manufactured goods came back. The road was a conduit of our national life.

Towns, counties, states had to build roads—and in turn the roads built them. As new portions of the national domain were surveyed, roads were laid out along the township and the section lines. We needed roads. We were the most mobile people in history, with the most bountiful natural resources any people had ever had. . . .

[1] From the introduction by Bernard DeVoto (1897-1956), critic, novelist, and editor, to *Freedom of the American Road*. Ford Motor Company. 3000 Schaefer Road. Dearborn, Michigan. 1956. p6-10. Reprinted by permission.

A highway is . . . a true index of our culture. Take the machinery that enables us to bridge a river which up to now had to be ferried, or to cut twenty miles of the distance from Here to There by taking the road easily through a tunnel whereas before it had to twist tortuously through a mountain range. It embodies developments in technology, invention, industrial progress, education, finance, and so many other things that our whole cultural heritage has gone into producing it.

There is no more fascinating experience than to watch the construction of a highway, and no more illuminating experience than to spend a few hours on a rise above one watching the most mobile people go by on their businesses and pleasures. One comes to perceive that the American road represents a way of life. It is a way of life to which we were committed by the most thorough-going of our social revolutions, the one initiated by the passenger automobile and the motor truck. In no other nation is the motorized transport of people and freight so interstitial in everyone's daily life, in his business, his diet, his solvency, his recreation, even in his day-dreams. But before that greatest of our revolutions began, we already owned the most extensive network of roads in the world. The trouble is that the revolution has been progressive and is still going on. The implications of the automobile have always outrun our ability to understand them. The necessities it has created have multiplied faster than we have kept up with them. Both our population and our wealth have increased at a greater rate than the most careful calculations had prepared us for. That fact is the most impressive evidence of the power of the American economic system. Yet it is the primary reason our highway system has grown increasingly inadequate. . . .

The lag between what our roads are and the necessities they must meet results from the unparalleled increase of our wealth, business, and leisure. We are only beginning to transform the highway pattern of a predominantly rural and agricultural nation to one adequate for a predominantly urban and industrial nation. We have not kept pace with the increase of our needs. Still less have we got ahead of them so that we could prepare for the needs of the future. But it is certain that we have got to get ahead of them or, like the giant Gulliver, we will find ourselves helplessly bound by a myriad small threads, each trivial in itself.

It was the President of the United States who spoke of the increasing lag in highways as having created a national crisis. The word "crisis" should frighten no one, though clearly it shocked many, who may have first perceived that the word was accurate when they saw in cold type the size of the sums proposed to overcome it. They were shocked because it is hard to translate abstract and general terms into concrete realizations. Everyone has it brought home to him that Something Has Got To Be Done when on his way back to town he gets caught in a Sunday traffic jam because the approach to town is a two-lane road which should have been a four-lane road ten years ago. It is harder to realize that road patterns many miles away have a direct influence on this two-lane approach to town.

Yet everyone's profanity at that Sunday clogging of inadequate roads is the sound first step. It brings the abstract into terms of the personal. A just analogy might be one of those rural counties of two generations back where there was a steady seepage of time, strength, and wealth because malaria was endemic. No one felt any sense of crisis till he himself came down with chills and fever. There came a time when the community realized that John Smith's chills and fever were everyone's loss, that Something Had To Be Done, and it began to spray the breeding places of mosquitoes.

We have got to make not successive short strides but a long leap forward. We have got to stop planning and building a highway system piecemeal, on a limited basis. We have got to convert our highway system into one whose parts are properly coordinated with one another, and the system we build now has got to be so planned that it can be rationally developed and proliferated with the expanding needs of the future.

It is a big job, a radical job. It is so big and so radical that it staggers the imagination; also it kindles the imagination. The cost will be enormous but also it will be infinitesimal, considering the wealth now being lost by seepage that it will save and the new wealth that it will create. The difficulties will also be enormous but they are precisely the kind of difficulties, and on precisely the same vast scale, that have always stimulated and exhilarated the American people. The job of building the first transcontinental railroad or the Panama Canal also staggered the imagination. There were plenty of prophets who predicted that both would bankrupt the nation and that neither could ever be completed. We took them in our stride.

Like charity, the building of roads begins at home. We are bound together in a vast national circuit or physiology. An impulse felt at Albany travels on to San Francisco, transport delayed at Brookville causes loss and irritation at Springville. Any large social action is the mixture of local, state, and Federal effort that is characteristically American, and the creation of a functional highway system will be just that. We assent amiably when we hear such phrases as "traffic planning" and "highway safety" but the need is to translate the ideas into individual, personal experience—my car or truck, the bus I travel on, my loss of time getting home, my expense through delay, my anxiety about my children's safety.

One of the threads that bind the giant's strength runs right past our door—in Brookville, Maine; Brookville, California, and all the Brookvilles in between. . . . The problem is national. Town joins town for three thousand miles; when you add Brookville to Brookville you get the necessity of the nation. It is the necessity of a nation which has developed technology far more fully than any other, and as a result is wealthier and more powerful than any other. We must now solve the problem of giving our culture the highways that its abundance demands.

It begins in front of our house but it will end by loosing the threads which bind the giant so that he can use his full strength —for the first time.

OUR HIGHWAY HISTORY [2]

When the first European colonists crossed the Atlantic to the New World, they found a wilderness threaded only by streams and Indian trails. The first settlements were built on the bays

[2] From *Highways in the United States*, pamphlet. United States Department of Commerce. Bureau of Public Roads. Washington 25, D.C. 1954. p 1-4.

and tidal rivers, where ships from across the sea could find safe harbor. As land close to the ocean was settled, new colonies moved inland along the navigable streams. Paths were cut through the forests, from the inland settlements to the ocean ports. Travel was mostly on foot or horseback, or in dugouts or birchbark canoes.

Before the Revolutionary War the white men had settled a strip of land 150 miles wide along the Atlantic sea coast. Close to the coast, roads connected the towns, but at best they were rutted wagon routes widened from pack trails and Indian paths. The westward links were only tracks through the woods. Much of the trade was carried by sailing sloop on the rivers.

One of the earliest overland routes in the American colonies was the Connecticut Path, an Indian trail from Boston through Springfield to Hartford. This was traveled in 1633 by emigrants from Boston, bound for settlement on the Connecticut River. Within a few years this route, and two alternates, reached to New Haven and on to New York. They became known as the Upper, Middle, and Lower Boston Post Roads. Post riders began carrying mail along the Post Road in 1673.

Gradually the colonies were connected with a continuous north-south route along the coast. In 1717, post riders carried mail once a month (in summer) along the six-hundred-mile route between Boston and Williamsburg, then capital of Virginia. Rapid public passenger service began in 1766 with the "Flying Machine," a box wagon which ran regularly from Camden, across the Delaware River from Philadelphia, to Paulus Hook (now Jersey City). Passengers ferried across the Hudson River to New York City. The ninety-mile trip took two days.

The Pennsylvania Road, a pathway from Philadelphia to the forks of the Ohio River (now Pittsburgh), became an important westward route from the Atlantic seaboard. A wagon road was built as far as Harrisburg, and extended beyond in 1758 by General [John] Forbes as a supply route in the campaign against Fort Duquesne.

One of the first carefully constructed roads in this country, built on engineering principles, was the Philadelphia-Lancaster Turnpike. This sixty-two-mile road, completed in 1796, had a twenty-four-foot wide crushed-stone surface, and cost $7,500 a mile. It marked the beginning of construction of all-weather roads.

The last half of the eighteenth century marked the change from foot or horseback travel to the more general use of coach and wagon. By 1802, freight-wagon and stage-coach lines were operating from Boston to Savannah. The twelve-hundred-mile trip took twenty-two and a half days by stage coach, at the "high" speed of fifty-three miles a day. Passengers stopped overnight at taverns along the way.

The need arose for surfaced roads. But the counties and towns could do little with the occasional labor of their citizens, given in place of road-tax payments. The states, poor and in debt after the heavy cost of the Revolutionary War, had no money for road improvement. The answer was found in turnpike companies which, with authority from the states, built and operated gravel or crushed-stone roads along the principal routes of travel. Tolls were collected on these turnpikes at gates set up along the way. For forty years, beginning about 1800, turnpikes were built everywhere in the east, and later throughout the midwest to the Mississippi River. There were four hundred in New York State alone. Stage-coach and freight-hauling lines increased rapidly during this period.

The Appalachian Mountains had been a barrier to the west. The first trail across the mountains was laid out in 1743 by the Ohio Company, to bring settlers into the rich Ohio River Valley. In 1775, Daniel Boone blazed the Wilderness Trail through the Cumberland Gap, near Middlesboro, Kentucky, to the fertile lands on the Ohio, Cumberland, and Kentucky Rivers.

Pioneers thronged the trails across the Appalachians. Between 1775 and 1800, probably three hundred thousand people passed through the Cumberland Gap on their way to the "west"— fifteen or twenty wagons every day during the open months. Beginning in 1806, the Federal Government undertook the improvement of one of the most important of these westward routes, extending at first from Cumberland, Maryland, westward to Wheeling, on the Ohio River. This road, known as the National Pike, was the first major road-building venture of the

Federal Government. After more than thirty years, the road had been extended into Illinois. It was intended to reach St. Louis, but the Government never completed it. Others [i.e. the states, with toll roads] took up the work, and after some years it finally reached the banks of the Mississippi.

Across the Wide Missouri

As the country beyond the Appalachians began to fill up, the hardier pioneers and traders, seeking new lands, pushed westward across the Mississippi and Missouri Rivers. In 1822, the Santa Fe Trail, starting at St. Louis, was opened to permit American trade with the newborn Republic of Mexico, to which all of the present southwestern United States then belonged. By 1842, the Oregon Trail carried a stream of emigrants from the banks of the Missouri across the Rocky Mountains to the Pacific northwest. The Mormons, seeking their promised land, pioneered the Mormon Trail from Nauvoo, Illinois, to the Great Salt Lake in 1847. The discovery of gold at Sutter's Mill in 1849 brought thousands more across the continent, along the Oregon Trail to the Rockies, and thence southwest on the California Trail.

These historic western trails were not really roads at all. The first pioneers set out in the general direction of their goal, wandering from their course to find shallow fords in the rivers and to avoid the badlands and deserts. Trappers and traders set out on foot, their provisions loaded on pack horses. Settlers followed in wagon trains, using the famous prairie schooners. Across the prairies the trails were simply wagon tracks through the grass. The lowest mountain passes in the Rockies were sought out, but the only road work done was to roll the rocks aside.

East of the Mississippi, most of the roads were rutted, winding tracks, dusty when dry and deep with mud in wet weather. Some of the turnpikes, between the larger cities, did have surfaces of broken stone. Bridges of timber or stone spanned the rivers, but the shallow streams were waded at fords. Travel was almost impossible in winter and early spring, and difficult enough in summer. But the population of the country was increasing, and commerce and agriculture needed improved roads. Everything pointed to a period of extensive highway construction.

Then, in 1829, the first steam locomotive in the United States was given a trial run. Within two years regular service was started on the Baltimore and Ohio Railroad. The railroad proved the best means of transportation over long distances. Canals, too, bid for passenger and freight business, and were successful for some years. The slow horse-drawn vehicles, with their small capacity, could not compete. The Conestoga wagon freight lines and the stage coaches went out of business. As tolls dropped off, the turnpike companies failed. Highway transportation in rural areas entered a long period of neglect.

From 1830 to 1890 there was a gradual increase in the total mileage of roads as the population of the country grew. But there was little improvement in their condition. Rural roads were entirely under the care of the counties and local governments. They had little money to spend for permanent improvement, even in such simple ways as building gravel or stone surfaces.

The Horseless Carriage Arrives

By 1890, lands away from the railroads had been settled, and farmers began to demand roads that could be traveled all year round. While the railroad could haul produce from a rural area to the big city, it was small help to the farmer if his loaded wagon got stuck in the mud on the way to the station.

About the same time the bicycle suddenly became a popular fad. Several million "wheelmen" called loudly for smoother roads, so they could enjoy their rides out into the country. As a result of these demands by the farmers and bicyclists, there began a nation-wide movement for improved highways.

There were about 2 million miles of rural highways in the United States in 1890, but almost all of them were dirt roads. Only about one hundred thousand miles had surfaces that could be used in all kinds of weather, and practically all of these were of gravel or crushed stone. Experiments with better types were being tried. The first brick pavement was laid in Charleston,

West Virginia, in 1872. Portland cement concrete was tried in Bellefontaine, Ohio, in 1893. Both of these were much too expensive for widespread use on rural roads at that time. Tests with oil and tar, in an attempt to curb the dust nuisance and to keep the gravel surfaces from breaking up, were the beginnings of our modern bituminous surfaces.

The good-roads movement swelled tremendously with the coming of the horseless carriage. It has continued without let-up ever since. The Duryea brothers built the first gasoline automobile in 1893. There were eight thousand automobiles in the United States in 1900, only seven years later. By 1925 there were 20 million motor vehicles on our roads and streets. . . .

The first step away from purely local support of roads came in 1891, when New Jersey began to provide state-aid money to its counties for road building. By 1900, six other states had passed similar laws, and every state had some kind of state aid to counties for roads by 1917.

Almost ninety years after the beginning of the building of the National Pike, the Federal Government resumed its interest in highways when, in 1893, the Congress created the Office of Road Inquiry in the Department of Agriculture. Its job was to study methods of road making, publish information on the subject, and build short "object-lesson" roads throughout the country.

Gradually the states entered further into highway work. The progress in most of them followed about the same pattern. At first a small office was created to control the use of state aid by the local governments. State and local funds were used in building the state-aid roads, but maintenance was often left to the counties. The final step was full state control of construction and maintenance of a state highway system by a state highway department. A few states began this movement before 1900. Many of them did not pass through the final stages until about 1920.

Aid from the Federal Government

The process might have taken longer if it had not been for a law, passed in 1916 by Congress, which began the policy of providing Federal-aid money to the states for road construction. The joint Federal-state highway construction program continues today in much the same way as it was started. The Federal-aid funds provided by Congress are divided among the states in proportion to their areas, populations, and mileage of rural mail routes. The money is used only for construction and must be matched by the states, in general with an equal amount of their own money. The states select the roads to be improved, and the type of improvement. They make the surveys and plans, and supervise the construction. In all these steps, when Federal-aid funds are used, the states consult with and obtain the approval of the Federal Government. The states are pledged to maintain the roads constructed with Federal aid. The Bureau of Public Roads, which had developed under several different names from the Office of Road Inquiry, acts for the Federal Government in the operation of the Federal-aid program. The Bureau is now a part of the Department of Commerce.

The 1916 law also required each state to have a state highway department if it wanted to receive Federal-aid funds. This greatly increased the importance of the then-existing state highway departments, and caused them to be created in those states where they had not yet been set up.

An important improvement in the Federal-aid policy was made in 1921 by a law which called upon the states to select a system of principal interstate and intercounty highways, limited (originally) to 7 per cent of the total mileage of rural roads then existing. Federal-aid money from then on could be used only on this system. This particular attention to a carefully selected group of important roads had a large influence in the rapid development of our nation-wide network of improved highways.

Facing the need, the states began carrying on large road construction programs. Industry and agriculture learned the value of motor truck transportation from the example shown by its use during the first World War. Trucks multiplied overnight. In the following years the passenger car advanced from a Sunday-ride luxury to an everyday part of living.

There was no expansion in the actual mileage of rural roads —the total of about 3 million miles was reached shortly after the

first World War and has not changed much since. But the surfaced mileage, which was only 387,000 miles in 1921, had increased a million miles by 1941.

In the 1920's the major effort was in answer to the cry of the
mud-bound farmers. Particularly on the state highway systems,
hard surfacing was the vital need—improvement of width,
grades, and curves seemed of lesser importance. Vehicles moved
slowly and traffic congestion was as yet unknown, but mud was
everywhere. So this policy was unquestionably right for the
times.

During the 1930's the states approached their original goal.
The important roads were surfaced. But in the meanwhile the
number of motor vehicles had increased tremendously. Speeds
were much higher. Trucks were bigger and carried heavier loads.
The highway builders began again, for the older surfaces were
wearing out and costing too much to maintain. In rebuilding,
they were made wider, stronger, smoother. Steep hills were cut
down; sharp curves were rounded; "blind" spots were improved
to give better sight distance.

It was in this period that study and planning became an important part of highway work. Led by the Bureau of Public
Roads, the states collected information on the extent, character,
and condition of the rural roads, the traffic using them, and the
methods by which they were financed. In later years, ways were
found to study city traffic, too. Study of all this information
helped the states to better understand their current highway problems and to forecast those of the future.

World War II

World War II halted the steps being taken to solve these
problems. Civilian travel was limited by gasoline rationing;
manufacture of new vehicles and tires was cut off. Yet the highways were called on to carry tremendous quantities of war goods
—timber and ore from forests and mines to processing points;
airplane wings and motors from factories to assembly plants;
cartridges and cannon from arsenals to seaports. Millions of
workers had to drive to work at these factories, many of them

newly built in corn fields miles from the city. The heavy loads of war traffic made wear and tear on the roads even worse than normal.

Yet materials and labor for highway work were severely limited, since little could be spared from the war effort. Construction could be done only on access roads leading into factories and military establishments, and on the most important highways which were vital to the movement of war goods, workers, and troops. Many miles of worn-out roads, scheduled for replacement, had to be kept in service by the limited means available. Transportation played a large part in winning the war, and the highways did their share. But the toll in damaged, neglected roads was heavy. And the normal program of replacement and improvement was snuffed out for three years.

Following the end of World War II, peacetime traffic quickly resumed its stride. Within a year it had broken prewar records, and has continued to grow ever since. The states were ready for a big road-building program. Plans were prepared and large amounts of state and Federal-aid money were available. But because of high prices and shortages of materials, men and machinery, the expected program did not get into high gear until about 1948. Meanwhile the mileage of roads no longer adequate for the traffic carried, or dangerous for present-day speeds, or difficult to keep in good condition, grew steadily larger. In cities everywhere, traffic was snarled and drivers snarling.

Much has been done. Three fifths of our 3 million miles of rural roads now have some kind of surface; and four fifths of our city streets. The states built or rebuilt 26,600 miles of their primary roads in 1952. The Federal, state, and local governments spent $5 billion in that year, constructing and operating our roads and streets. But we are a long way yet from keeping pace with the growth of traffic.

Careful review of our highway situation, and study of what we may expect in the future, show that we face five general problems. Relief for the huge traffic volumes on main routes approaching and inside the cities, and more parking space, are the most urgent problems. Next is the improvement to high standards of the most important routes connecting the principal cities and industrial centers. To provide general highway service, the larger network of main highways must be modernized. And the needs of the farmers require the improvement of a well-selected system of secondary roads, linked to the main highway network.

OUR ROADS TODAY [3]

Of the 3,003,000 miles of rural roads in the United States today, almost 358,000 are included in the primary state highway systems. These are the main routes, carrying most of the traffic, and they reach every city in the United States.

About 2,567,000 miles are secondary roads that serve the land and connect the farms and the countless hamlets and cross-roads settlements with the main highways. The counties have control of 1,739,000 miles of these secondary roads, and the town and township governments have control of 622,000 miles. In recent years, some states have taken over many or all of the secondary roads within their borders. The total of secondary roads under state control is now 206,000 miles. The states have 8,000 miles of roads in state forests and parks, also.

The Federal Government has some 70,000 miles of national forest, national park, and Indian reservation roads under its control. These, by the way, are the only roads built and maintained wholly by the Federal Government. The United States has no national highway system such as there are in many other countries.

The 319,000 miles of city streets and highways in the United States are largely under the control of the cities themselves. There are about 33,000 miles of principal streets, which serve as connections for the state highways, that are controlled by the state highway departments.

Out of the 3,322,000 miles of roads and streets in our country, the most important ones, about 145,000 miles of them, are numbered and marked with the well-known U S shield. This U S numbered system has nothing to do with the control of the roads. There are no particular funds for the system, and no special laws

[3] From *Highways in the United States*, pamphlet. United States Department of Commerce. Bureau of Public Roads. Washington 25, D.C. 1954. p5-7.

apply to it. It is an arrangement by the states, begun in 1928, to provide a convenient and simple way to guide travelers from city to city across the country. It is a very practical and useful system, indeed.

The Federal-Aid Systems

The Federal-aid systems do not include any roads that have not already been described: They are made up of roads which are parts of the state and local systems. While Federal-aid funds are used in building these roads, they remain under the control of the state and local governments to which they belong.

The oldest of the systems is the Federal-aid highway system, of which the rural portion, called the Federal-aid primary system, was first laid out by the states and the Bureau of Public Roads in 1921. It has, of course, been changed somewhat from time to time as the needs of traffic have changed. The Federal-aid highway system includes 234,837 miles of roads and streets, of which 219,196 miles are rural roads. They are the most important rural state highway routes.

The remainder of the Federal-aid highway system, called the Federal-aid urban system, is made up of 15,641 miles of city streets. These are the connections of the state highway routes through cities, and other principal city traffic arteries. During the first twenty years of Federal aid, the main effort was to get the rural roads surfaced. In the depression of the 1930's, some Federal help was given to cities for highways, in order to make useful jobs for people who were out of work. Congress first began to provide Federal-aid funds specifically for urban highways in the Federal-aid law of 1944. The state highway departments handle these urban Federal-aid funds, but of course they work in cooperation with the cities.

Relatively small amounts of Federal aid had been provided since 1933 for secondary or farm-to-market roads. The Federal-aid law of 1944 called for the selection of a Federal-aid secondary system, and the larger amounts of Federal money now provided for secondary roads must be used on this system. The routes in the system are the most important secondary roads, feeding traffic from farms and villages into the main highways and to the market centers. They were chosen by the states, the local governments, and the Bureau of Public Roads, working together. The system now has 416,989 miles of rural roads. Most of them are county or local government roads, but some are in the primary and secondary road systems controlled by the states.

Included in the Federal-aid highway system is the National System of Interstate Highways, perhaps the most important of all. This Interstate System was created by the 1944 law, after its need was clearly shown by several careful studies by the state highway departments and the Bureau of Public Roads. The system is limited by law to 40,000 miles [increased to 41,000 miles by the Federal-Aid Highway Act of 1956]. Its routes were selected by the states and the Bureau of Public Roads, and are the most heavily traveled in the country. They connect all of the major cities and production centers of the United States. The National System of Interstate Highways is a part of the larger Federal-aid highway system, and the regular Federal-aid funds are used for its improvement.

The operation of the Federal-aid program under the supervision of the Bureau of Public Roads has already been described. The Bureau has its main office in Washington. In order to work closely with the state highway departments, the Bureau has ten division offices across the country, and a small district office in each state. The Bureau works in close cooperation with the state highway departments. Aside from its job of handling the Federal-aid program, the Bureau also builds roads for the Federal Government, mostly in national parks and forests.

The Bureau, as one of its major responsibilities, conducts an extensive program in all phases of highway research. Far from being abstract, this research is an important tool in administrative and technical progress. The Highway Research Board, the state highway departments, universities, and other organizations also do much highway research work.

The Bureau is now operating extensively overseas, giving technical aid to countries that have had little experience in modern highway practice. It has provided funds and engineers to the Central American republics to help survey and build the Inter-American Highway, and to the Philippines for rehabilitation of its war-destroyed roads and bridges. Bureau engineers are advising the highway departments in several South American countries, in Turkey, Ethiopia, and Liberia. Other countries are now seeking its technical aid.

The State Highway Departments

Every state has a highway department, which handles the construction, maintenance, and management of the state highway system. These are the most important and the best organized and equipped road-building agencies of the nation. Most states are divided into districts so that the men who supervise the construction and maintenance work will be closer to it. The top management of the highway departments varies among the states: fourteen of them are run by one executive, usually called the commissioner; twenty-eight are supervised by a group of men, or commission; and six have both an executive and a commission.

The departments employ many engineers. But they also have accountants, lawyers, real-estate experts, draftsmen, stenographers, and clerks. Many of the engineers are specialists in a particular kind of highway work, such as road or bridge design, surveying, traffic, maintenance, materials, soils, etc. Some of them work at research or testing of materials.

While the highway departments design the road and bridge projects, they generally hire contractors to do the actual building. Usually each job is advertised, and contractors send in their bids. The one who offers to do the work for the least money gets the job, if he is responsible and capable. During construction, highway department engineers stay at the job to see that it is done properly.

Maintenance of state highways is done largely by employees of the state highway department. This is a big job. It means patching broken pavement, putting bituminous coatings on rough surfaces, painting bridges and traffic stripes, cutting weeds, planting trees, removing snow, setting up traffic signs and signals, operating draw bridges and ferries, and many other kinds of repair and upkeep. This housekeeping of the existing highways is just as important to the motorist as the building of new roads.

The Local Rural Roads

More than 18,000 local governmental units have an interest of some kind in the local rural roads. These include 2,750 counties, 14,500 towns and townships, and 950 special road districts. In New England the local roads are largely controlled by the towns, and in Pennsylvania by the townships. In the southern and western states the counties generally handle local road affairs. In the rest of the country, with some exceptions, the counties have charge of the more important local roads and the townships take care of the remainder. The townships in a few states have voluntarily handed over their road responsibilities to the counties. Some states have taken the more heavily traveled local roads into their state highway systems, and in Delaware, North Carolina, Virginia (except in three counties), and West Virginia all rural roads are under state control.

The local road units vary in size from little districts only a mile square to California's San Bernardino County, which is bigger than New Hampshire and Vermont put together. The road systems these local governments control range from less than five miles to more than five thousand miles in length. The money they have to spend for highway work varies from $500 to more than $10 million a year. The size of their highway units runs all the way from a single part-time worker to organizations with more than five hundred employees.

Many of the local highway departments, particularly the larger ones, operate in much the same way as do the state highway departments. Since a large part of their road systems are earth or gravel, they do a good deal of construction with their own men and machinery. Those that are properly manned and equipped do an excellent job in maintaining the local roads.

Some of the smaller local road units, however, are not so efficiently operated or well managed. They have small mileages of roads to maintain, and so cannot afford specialized machinery or an engineering staff. There are several possible solutions to these problems. State-aid and Federal-aid secondary road funds help the local governments financially. Many of the state highway departments have special staffs of engineers to advise the counties and townships in highway planning and building. In recent years some of the local units have pooled their work, in groups of two or more, so as to make better use of equipment and skilled employees. All of these efforts toward better local road management have been encouraged by the Federal Government through the Federal-aid laws.

The Cities

There are about seventeen thousand cities, boroughs, and villages that are engaged in construction and maintenance of the streets and highways within their limits. Like the local rural governments, the size and nature of their work varies greatly—from the little village with a few blocks of "Main Street" to the great cities like New York and Chicago. In many states the cities receive state-aid funds, and in some states the principal streets carrying the state highway routes into and through the cities are under state control. The most important streets are often on the Federal-aid urban system and can be improved with Federal-aid funds.

City streets, like rural roads, are of varying degrees of importance. The main thoroughfares, radiating like the spokes of a wheel, bring traffic into the business and industrial centers from the intercity and interstate highways and from the nearby suburbs. Important cross-town streets connect these spokes, linking the different parts of the city. The remainder of the streets provide local service to residential areas.

The city highway departments have the same basic work to do as the counties and townships, or the state highway departments. They build, repair, and control traffic on the streets. But in the larger cities the work is difficult and complicated. Traffic is very heavy, especially during the morning and evening hours when people are going to and from work. Most of the streets have to be paved with hard surfaces. They are subject to terrific wear, and are frequently cut into for repair of underground facilities like sewer, water, and gas pipes, and electric and telephone wires. Street-car and bus lines, and the loading and unloading of trucks, are complications the rural governments do not have to deal with. To keep traffic moving as smoothly as possible, cities need many traffic signals and police officers. In the very large cities, the modern expressway, which eliminates cross traffic, is the only solution to traffic congestion on the major thoroughfares. . . . [For a detailed account of city street and traffic problems, the reader is referred to *Community Planning* (Reference Shelf, Volume 28, Number 4), edited by Herbert L. Marx, Jr.—Ed.]

is a popular idea that main highways should by-pass the cities. A lot of traffic goes in one side and comes out the other, so why not take it around? Traffic studies of origin and destination reveal, however, that the vehicles coming out are not the same ones that go in on the other side. Many of them stay in the city, or at least stop for a while, and relatively few go right through. For instance, in cities of 25,000 to 50,000 population, about 22 per cent of the vehicles want to go through. About 30 per cent head for the central business district, and the remainder are bound for some other part of the city. And the larger the city, the larger the proportion of traffic that wants to stop. Thus the main highways will serve traffic best if they enter all but the smallest cities and skirt the area of the central business district. In the smallest urban places, it is desirable to locate the by-pass as close as possible to the city.

The tremendously heavy volume of traffic entering and leaving the central parts of a large city is partly from the rural highways and partly from the suburbs. There is a regular tide of movement, coming to work in the morning and going home at night. Expressways are needed for this traffic. These are divided highways, with two or more lanes each way and a separating strip between. Entrance and exit is allowed only at selected places, with ramps and overpasses or underpasses arranged so that vehicles do not have to cross in front of each other. There are no traffic lights or cross streets.

Expressways often cost several million dollars a mile. This is not only because they are expensive to build, but also because they take a lot of valuable land. Years ago, narrow streets were sufficient for the slow, small wagons and carriages that used them. Now, to widen these streets and make them into expressways, it is often necessary to tear down block after block of buildings. But in spite of the heavy cost, expressways are certainly justified and several of our big cities are building them. Without enough expressways and parking space to make it easy for traffic to get downtown and stop there, business suffers. It has already suffered a good deal. Many shopping centers have developed in outlying areas which are easily reached from the suburbs and where parking space can be provided.

The Condition of Our Highways

Of the 3,343,000 miles of rural roads and city streets in the United States, 1,273,000 miles are unimproved or graded and drained dirt roads. Another 1,216,000 miles are surfaced with stabilized soil or with gravel or crushed stone. Only 854,000 miles, or a little more than one fourth of the total, are "paved" in the sense commonly understood. Of these, 454,000 miles have low-type bituminous (tar or asphalt) surfaces, and 400,000 are high-type bituminous, Portland cement concrete, brick, or stone block. Many of these surfaces are far from being new or adequate. More than 126,000 miles of the surfaced primary state rural highways are less than twenty feet wide; only 4,000 miles are divided highways of four or more lanes. Such statistics show what every motorist knows: that much of our road and street mileage is satisfactory but much of it is inadequate for present-day traffic.

To trace the progress that has taken place in road improvement, the development of the state primary rural system of highways provides a good indication. These highways are continuous routes that join the major cities of the nation and also connect many of the county seats. Included in this system are most of the U S numbered routes, the Federal-aid primary rural system, and the heavily traveled routes of the National System of Interstate Highways. While these primary state roads represent only 12 per cent of the total rural mileage in the United States, they carry 73 per cent of all rural traffic.

In 1930, about 30 per cent of the 324,000 miles of the state primary rural system were dirt roads. By 1952 the system had grown to 371,000 miles and nearly all of the roads have an all-weather surface. The small portion of unsurfaced mileage remaining in the system includes roads on which grading has been accomplished for the eventual surfacing. In a few states, the system includes a limited mileage of unsurfaced roads that does not justify, in terms of traffic or traffic potential, the cost of immediate improvement.

Most of the growth in the system has taken place since 1937. A large part of the increase has resulted from transfer of roads from local governments to state responsibility. Mileage built on new location has also been a contributing factor. In the sixteen-year period, miles of road-building accomplished equals in total the number of miles in the system in 1937. In other words, the work completed during the period was the equivalent of resurfacing every mile in the system as it existed in 1937.

What has happened to the surfaces on these roads over the sixteen-year period? The former dirt roads and many miles of those having gravel or other low-type surfaces have been improved, for the most part, with the addition of bituminous materials. Many miles of old Portland cement concrete and brick surfaces that had given long years of service have been resurfaced with a bituminous mat. This practice is an economical method of improving a road by retaining the good qualities of the old road as a base for the new surface. Where it is necessary to completely rebuild an existing road or, because of poor alignment, relocation is required, concrete or high-type bituminous surfaces are generally built.

What types of roads are being built today on these main thoroughfares? Of the 26,600 miles built or rebuilt during 1952, more than one half of the roads were constructed with high-type surfaces, about one third with intermediate types, and the remainder with low-type surfaces such as gravel, stone, or slag.

How wide are these highways built? About 95 per cent of the primary roads constructed provide two traffic lanes. The remaining 5 per cent are designed for additional capacity. The construction of divided highways having four or more traffic lanes accounts for only 2 per cent of the total mileage built on primary rural highways. The mileage of divided highways constructed seems astoundingly small, but studies have shown that traffic in relatively few rural areas requires building according to the modern concept of the superhighway. In most instances, the two-lane highway built to modern standards has sufficient capacity to carry present traffic as well as that anticipated during the life expectancy of the roadway. Where traffic growth is expected in the near future, two-lane roads are built with right-of-way reserved to accommodate extra lanes as the need arises. Highways connecting large metropolitan areas require, however, the construction of the divided highway designed to carry the heavy flow of traffic at greater speeds and with greater safety.

THE GREAT TRANSFORMATION [4]

There are in the United States many thousands of villages and towns served only by highway and motor vehicle.

These communities have all the comforts of modern civilization. Their groceries, their clothing, their medicine, their magazines and newspapers arrive regularly on rubber tires. The things the town makes—barrels, blankets, or paper boxes—go out to the world on rubber tires.

If the people in the town want to go anywhere, they don't miss the railroad station. They simply get in their automobiles, start them up, and go someplace. . . .

When you have an entire nation of 165 million people going someplace, you're bound to change things.

Take a city of a million people built for carriages and street cars, with its narrow streets and packed-in population. Add 200,000 automobiles, and the city will never again be the same. Buildings will come down, streets will widen, and folks will move out into the surrounding country. Stores will move to new places. Little corner stores that served the walking shopper will give way to larger stores that serve the riding shopper. Add it all up, and it amounts to an explosion in slow motion, with our

    [4] From *A Car-Traveling People,* pamphlet by Franklin M. Reck, author and highway consultant. Automobile Manufacturers Association. New Center Building. Detroit 2, Michigan, 1955. Reprinted by permission.

worried city fathers picking up the pieces as fast as they can, and rearranging them in a newer and better pattern.

Take the country. We built our villages about seven miles apart, so that no farmer would have to go more than three or four miles to reach the general store and the feed mill. But even that was too far to go regularly, so stores and one-room schools began to appear at the crossroads, right out in the open country. Since the farmer couldn't get to town, the store, the school, and the church went out to the farmer.

Now add automobiles. Give one to practically every farmer, and give him a surfaced road to ride on. What happens? He drives right past the crossroads store and goes to the village. If he doesn't like the merchandise there, he drives on to the county seat, maybe twenty miles away. Open-country churches, one-room schools, and crossroads stores are boarded up and abandoned. The loneliness of farm life disappears. Differences in clothing and speech disappear too. You have to look hard, past the well-cut store clothing, at the tanned skin and calloused palm, to be able to say: "There's a farmer."

Take our medium-sized towns, the strong backbone of American life. At the turn of the century, Main Street was crowded on the Fourth of July. Flags flying, a parade, and fireworks in the park. The celebration had to be in town because it was so hard to go anywhere.

Today, Main Street is deserted on the Fourth. The folks are all out in the country with their kids.

Vacations once required planning. The family had to take a train to some beach or lake. It was something to be done only once a year, with cottages reserved in advance.

Now that we have automobiles, we turn every Sunday into a vacation. We go weekending to lakes, state parks, and relatives in the country. When it comes to the annual two weeks, we get into our cars and go wandering like the Arabs, all over the land.

Many of our highways, once dirt roads, are now concrete and macadam. Strange new sights transform the placid rural countryside. Trailer camps. Elaborate motor courts. Gas stations. Eating stands. Drive-in ice cream parlors. As the vacationer drives along he finds that the highway has become a great open-air arcade. If he travels far enough he can buy melons, eggs, fruit, chickens, vegetables, lawn chairs, weather vanes, pottery, sun dials, peanuts, golf hats and fishworms.

Take the geography of our country, itself. For 125 years we grew up, first along our rivers, then along our railroads. Thriving towns come into existence at the confluence of rivers, served by steamboat and barge, and inland ports mushroomed on the Great Lakes. Farther west, unrolling rails sliced through the plains, deserts, and mountains, leaving towns in their wake.

Now add 51 million automobiles and put down over the map of the United States a system of highways like an immense fishnet. Little hamlets, once doomed to sleepy isolation, come to life. Tiny black dots on the map grow larger and new dots appear where no rails and rivers pass.

Thousands of towns have declared their independence. They have learned to depend on rubber tires alone.

Background

When we talk about the changes the automobile has made in our lives, the year 1919 is a pretty good year to begin with. Nineteen-nineteen is important for a lot of reasons.

For one thing, 1919 was the first full year after World War I, when people could get down to making and buying the things they really wanted. How eagerly they wanted their own cars is fairly well proved by the figures. At the beginning of 1919 we had about 6 million automobiles, which seemed like a lot, but just ten years later we were to own 23 million! You might say that 1919 was the year before the deluge.

Then again, it was in 1919 that people finally decided, once and for all, that automobiling was more than a recreation. It was a necessity. It was part of their earning power. It was the way they wanted to travel to their jobs, do the shopping, and go to the dentist. It was the way they wanted to call on their prospects, selling hairpins, life insurance, and steel bridges.

So they began demanding closed cars, in order to travel about in winter as well as summer. A few short years after 1919, the open car was to become a rare animal. Then, too, the automobile manufacturer was giving folks other conveniences that helped make the car an all-year-round, day-and-night proposition. By 1919, people were getting used to self-starters and electric lights. They were getting demountable rims. The backaches were disappearing from automobiling.

By 1919, folks were deciding that touring was an inexpensive way of seeing their own nation. They even wrote books about it. One book told how a family of five could travel from Bemidji, Minnesota, to Kansas City on a sixteen-day vacation at a cost of $101.03, as compared with $921 by train. Free from war duties, folks were pouring out of the cities in automobiles loaded down with tents, cookstoves, fishing tackle, and groceries. . . .

You might say that 1919 was the beginning of the modern automobile age. It marked the passing of the linen duster, visored cap, and goggles. It marked the beginning of the greatest car-and-highway building age the world has ever seen. . . . The automobile came along and gave us something we had never completely posessed before. It gave us a sense of freedom, a feeling of independence, a means of escape from the monotony of our day-by-day surroundings. . . . When a farm wife was asked by a United States Department of Agriculture investigator why the family owned a car when it didn't own a bathtub, the woman replied with surprise:

"Why, you can't go to town in a bathtub."

Rural Transformation

Not so long ago, it was a serious matter for a farmer to get sick. It might be several hours before the doctor could drive to the home in his horse and buggy. A hard rain or a heavy snow might hold him up even longer. If the illness turned out to be something serious like acute appendicitis, the chances are that the doctor, when he *did* arrive, cleared off the kitchen table, lit all the available lamps, and went to work. . . .

Nothing illustrates the transformation of rural America from loneliness to community living better than the change in rural doctoring. . . .

In 1919, when Dr. P. A. Scheurer entered the practice of medicine in Manchester, Michigan, there were six doctors to care for the town of one thousand people and the surrounding countryside.

Dr. Scheurer started out in practice with a pair of horses and a rig. In those days the town had fifteen practical nurses to care for patients in their homes. People didn't go to hospitals much. The nearest large hospital was in Jackson, twenty-one miles away. Now and then, Dr. Scheurer attempted to take patients to Jackson or Ann Arbor in his rig, and there were times when the patient died during the trip.

In 1919, Dr. Scheurer purchased a Model T. Because of the condition of the roads he could use the car only in the summer when the weather was dry. In the winter, or in muddy weather, he relied on horses. He built up such a large practice with his flivver in summer that he needed a stable of six horses to maintain his practice in the winter.

In 1920, he bought a sedan, his first experience with a closed car. By this time roads were good enough so that he used his car most of the time, traveling 12,000 miles a year and using horse and buggy only in very bad weather.

In 1925, he got rid of his horses altogether and sold his cutter and rig. Now and then, he regretted the passing of the horse. In winter, when snow covered the county roads, he would drive as far as the main highways took him and there the farmer would meet him with a sleigh to take him the rest of the way.

By 1942, Dr. Scheurer was putting 35,000 miles a year on his car. His name was known for some fifty miles in all directions. He was on the staff of three hospitals and could reach all of them in a forenoon. He would go to the Saline Hospital fifteen miles away, travel from there the twenty-two miles to Tecumseh, go on for thirty-two miles to the Mercy Hospital in Jackson, and return the twenty-one miles to Manchester—all by one o'clock. In the afternoon and evening, some thirty-five to forty patients would call at his office, many of them drawn from a distance of fifty miles by his reputation.

By 1942 the automobile had completed its transformation of medical practice. There was not a single practical nurse in Manchester and kitchen operations were unknown. The town had an ambulance and a patient could be taken to any one of several hospitals within an hour, there to have the safeguards of a blood bank, oxygen and X-ray equipment, and adequate operating facilities. The six doctors of 1909 had dwindled to two and the two provided better service and made a better living than the six.

What has happened in Manchester has happened all over the country. Nearly half the doctors in small villages have disappeared because they're no longer needed. Many small, poorly equipped hospitals have closed up in favor of better hospitals in nearby larger towns. With good roads, automobiles, and ambulances, a patient today can ride thirty miles more safely than he could three miles in the old days.

The Automobile Takes Over Rural Mail

When the farmer comes in from the field for his noonday meal, the chances are there's a big-city daily paper on the table. There may also be a seed catalog, a farm journal, a letter from a far-away son. The daily mail delivery may include a large package from a mail order house or a tractor repair part, sent parcel post.

Rural delivery existed before the automobile, but the car made it a lot better. The car gave more service with fewer carriers. It delivered more tons of mail with less fuss.

In 1920 . . . the average rural mail route was 26.5 miles . . . [and] we needed 43,445 rural mail carriers to cover 1,151,832 miles of rural route.

By 1954 the average route was 47 miles. We needed only 32,370 carriers to cover 1,521,014 miles of rural route. Not only that, but we carried more tons of letters, daily papers, magazines, and packages; we raised the salaries of mail carriers; we cut down the time they spent on the road. And with all these improvements, we actually cut down the annual per-mile cost of rural mail service. . . .

The doctor's car delivered a body blow to farm illness. The mail carrier's car delivered a body blow to farm loneliness. The motor car was truly a liberating force.

Goodbye Isolation

Isolation is the word for it.

It means living alone, seldom seeing anyone, seldom going any place. Just plowing, washing and ironing, cooking, and milking from dawn to dark; then tumbling into bed, sleeping the sleep of exhaustion, and getting up the next morning to face the same round of work.

Isolation was inevitable when you consider how our countryside grew. In our hunger for land, we Americans didn't develop as did rural people in Europe, where villages were close together and farmers lived in the village by night and worked their farms by day. Our people went out to the land and built their homes on it. They lived in simple frame houses maybe a mile, maybe two miles, from the nearest neighbor.

A man could face this life better than a woman. He would become wrapped up in his crops, his stock, his land, and forget the rest. But the woman of the farm thought of her children, and she worried about many things. About what to do if a chest cold developed, or a fever rash showed on Tommy's face. She wanted to know more about the rules of health and diet.

She wanted new ideas for curtains in the parlor, and what kind of wallpaper would go best in the bedroom if they ever redecorated. She wanted to know more about the new ways of canning foods.

The cry for help that went up from farm women is something our parents remember better than we. It was like an S.O.S. from a ship at sea.

The answer came in an automobile driven by a home demonstration agent. She was from the nearest agricultural college, a specialist of the Extension Service trained in home economics.

Home demonstration started out in a small way and grew and grew. As cars and highways improved, it grew faster and faster. Each home demonstration agent picked likely farm women and trained them as leaders. These volunteer leaders, in turn, put on shows at meeting halls, or in farm homes. They held cooking schools, health schools, canning demonstrations, house furnishing and landscape gardening programs.

In 1920 there were less than 1,000 home demonstration agents and less than 50,000 leaders. By 1954, with better highways and better cars, there were 3,005 agents and 600,000 leaders.

Farm wives get into their cars and drive long distances to attend home demonstration meetings. In crowded eastern states their round trips average seven miles, in central states thirteen miles, and in the West, twenty-four. A Nevada woman wrote: "Some of us go thirty-five miles one way," and an Oregon woman stated that trips of one hundred and twenty-five miles to county-wide meetings were common.

You can hardly imagine all this happening without automobiles and highways. The home demonstration agent has been described by one farm woman as "Heaven come to earth in a Tin Lizzie."

Home demonstration was another body blow to rural isolation.

Science Rides to the Farm

Home making isn't all that rode to the farm in an automobile.

So did better farming. What the farm husband wanted to know was how to get more bushels per acre. More pounds of meat per bushel of feed, fewer crop failures, less trouble with pests.

Today, the sight of farmers' cars parked alongside a field, with the men grouped around a planting of hybrid corn or a lime demonstration, is common. The man in the center of the group is the county agent, bringing the wisdom of the college experiment station out to the farmer.

You'd expect county agent work to grow, along with the improvement of automobiles and highways, and it has. The number of county agents jumped from 2,000 in 1920 to 6,100 in

1955. Attendance at farm meetings leaped from 12 million per year to 75 million in the same time.

While this work with grownups was going on, the 4-H Clubs for farm boys and girls were growing to a membership of 2.1 million.

That's the way a planned campaign for better farm living was accelerated by automobiles. To carry on a program like that, folks had to get around.

We doubt if any city person appreciates his automobile as a farmer does. The farm car is a work car.

An agricultural expert once figured the ways in which a farmer uses his passenger car. The list went something like this:

"Haul butter, cream, produce, poultry, eggs, and fruit to market. Fetch repair parts, fertilizer, seed, hardware, and spray materials from town. Saw wood, using a belt attachment. Haul labor from town to farm and from one part of the farm to another. Round up stock. Haul implements on the road."

Farms today are powered by internal combustion engines. Men plow, cultivate, put hay in the barn, load silos, and chop feed, all by gasoline power. This means frequent trips to welding shop and garage for repair parts. The passenger car makes these trips. It provides the necessary link to keep the internal-combustion farm running.

The more you study the work a farm car performs, the more interesting the picture is. Down South, tobacco farmers look over the day's markets to find which one is paying the best price. Then they load their leaf into a trailer, hitch it on behind the automobile, and drive to that market.

As farmers got used to going places on surfaced highways, some of them began to figure that son Bill and daughter Jane might as well go to the town school where more and better courses were offered. So hauling the youngsters to school became another chore of the farm car, and after a while school buses came along to take the load. This is one of the reasons why one-room schools out in the country are disappearing at the rate of eight to nine a day.

In fact, one-room schools in this country have dropped from 200,000 in 1915-16 to 113,600 in 1939-40 and 50,000 in 1955, and it is no accident that this drop occurred in the years of the great growth of the automobile.

It's the same way with open-country churches and general stores out at the crossroads. Those two institutions served a great purpose in their day. Because of bad roads and distances, the farmer couldn't get to town to shop or to worship. So the church and store came out to him.

Now those fine pioneer institutions are disappearing along with the one-room country school. On Sunday mornings, the farmer's car is parked in front of the town church.

You could write a whole book about the changing shopping habits of the farmer and his wife. Once they shopped at the nearest general store because it was the only place they could get to. Now, if they don't like what's there, they go on to the village.

They even go farther. When it comes to a suit of clothes, or furniture, where the shopper likes to make a selection, the farmer may pass up the village store with its limited line, and drive right on to the big city.

You see, in the old days, the general store was a kind of monopoly based on nearness. You took what the general store offered, or did without. Then the automobile arrived and killed that monopoly by giving the farmer freedom to shop over a territory of twenty to fifty miles.

Summary of Changes

When you add all these changes together . . . you become aware that what has gradually happened amounts to a revolution in rural life.

Primitive, frontier medical service is all but gone from the scene and modern hospitalization has taken its place. Crossroads stores have lost trade to the village, and the village has lost trade to the county seat. With freedom to shop, farm folks dress in the current national fashion. With freedom to get about, farm youngsters go to the movies about as often as city youngsters. From the movies and from television they learn a universal diction, national styles, national manners. The outward differences that fostered the snobwords, "rube" and "city slicker," have broken down.

With freedom to get around, farm folks go to dinners, parties, picnics, school operettas, and chamber of commerce meetings. A rural social life has developed, and the center of that life is in village and town.

The surfaced highway and the car have centralized farm living. Fewer and better stores. Fewer and better schools. Fewer and better hospitals. More daily contacts. More fun in living. With the car, isolation and loneliness went out of date. . . .

New Kinds of Recreation

The automobile has changed our vacation and weekend habits about as much as it has transformed the pattern of rural and city life. [For its effect on city life the reader should consult *Community Planning* (Reference Shelf, Volume 28, Number 4), edited by Herbert L. Marx, Jr.—Ed.] Even before 1919 the touring vacation was born. We became nomads on rubber tires.

In 1919, a long tour was hazardous adventure. Highway signs were few, and most of us traveled by the Blue Book, which told us to ride out of Hicksville on Main Street, go 4.6 miles, turn right at the Baptist Church, continue 3.1 miles to the grain elevator, and turn left. Roads were bad, and an average of twenty-five miles an hour was good. Two hundred miles in a day was more than fair. If we had motor trouble we were lucky to get service.

People who were hardy enough to take transcontinental tours in 1919 generally allowed themselves thirty days for the trip, one way, and carried along such accessories as chains, tow rope, and a shovel.

These were the pioneers, the motorized Daniel Boones. Mostly, our long-distance tourists shipped their cars to the Pacific by rail, while eastern owners who wintered in Florida sent their automobiles south on coastwise steamers.

Those of us with less money to spend were pouring out onto the highways with tents, stoves, and luggage piled high in the back seat or loaded into two-wheel trailers.

These early tourists formed organizations for mutual help and advice. One such organization called itself the Tin Can Tourists' Association, and the identifying mark was a tin can perched on the radiator cap.

Something had to be done to accommodate the flood of motor campers, and at first towns set aside camping areas. Then a few enterprising farmers began to build cabins, and before long tourist courts blossomed out. In 1922, according to the American Automobile Association, there were some 600 tourist courts. By 1940, we had in this country 13,521 courts and camps doing an annual business of $37 million. Along with courts and camps, tourist homes came into existence to serve the traveler. Before the war, an estimated 50,000 homes rented rooms to tourists.

As tourist courts competed for trade the modern motel came into existence, often with restaurants and swimming pools, the rooms air-conditioned and containing radios and television sets. There were nearly 55,000 motels in 1955, doing a business of $1.5 billion.

Our new habit of taking tours had its effect on older institutions. Hotels suffered. Resorts that used to book vacationers for two weeks or a whole summer, found themselves transient hotels, entertaining guests for a night. Many went out of business altogether. Certain railroads serving vacation spots lost 80 per cent of their business to the automobile.

With motels increasing by the year, roads getting better all the time, and gas stations springing into being wherever they were needed, we began as a people to discover our continent for the first time.

Only 128,000 cars entered our national parks in 1920. Year by year the number grew until it hit 2 million cars in 1940. Of the 37 million people who visited national parks and monuments in 1951, over nine tenths of them went by car. It isn't too much to say that the automobile gave the mass of people their first chance to see the tall plume of Old Faithful, the spires of Bryce Canyon, and the wooded ridges of the Smokies. The car made the natural wonders of our nation the property of many, not just the privileged few.

We Visit Canada

The car gave us a chance to get acquainted with our neighbors, too. The way tourist travel to Canada has increased proves it. It was 128,696 cars in 1921. It was 2,506,000 in 1953. That's on two-day to thirty-day permits, not just daylight trips to a border city.

Mexico too. Through one port, Laredo, the entry of cars has increased from 6,362 automobiles in 1937 to 44,176 in 1951. Travel to Mexico over her fine new highways totaled 100,000 automobiles in 1954.

Yes, we're getting around and seeing our neighbors. In 1954 over 100,000 cars took the long graveled highway into the heart of Alaska, to see how folks live in our northernmost territory and to fish and hunt in the unspoiled woods and lakes along the way.

More important even than these ambitious trips to national parks and neighboring countries is the freedom the automobile has given us to visit the vacation spots near home. . . .

Few of us can afford transcontinental trips every year. Most of us seek a resort within a radius of five hundred miles. But within these five hundred miles the automobile has given us freedom of selection. Resorts have departed from the railroad and located themselves at the trailhead. Resorts can now be anywhere there's a road.

One way many of us find recreation these days is to make weekend trips to state parks. State parks, in fact, owe their existence to the automobile. Before cars took to the highways in great numbers there were hardly any state parks in the country.

Massachusetts, for example, had only one state park in 1920, and seven in 1942. California began its park system in 1927, Virginia in 1936, Missouri in 1925. Today there are about 2,000 state parks and scenic areas, with 166 million visitors reported in 1954. They offer horseback riding, nature hikes, swimming, speedboat rides and many other vacation activities.

Some states have gone even farther. They have not only built state parks but are trying to make their main rural highways one continuous park.

Michigan has been a leader in this development. Beginning with weed control and progressing to the laying of sod and planting of shrubs, Michigan has placed picnic tables, stoves, and water fountains at intervals along the highway, encouraging travelers to eat picnics under a tree. At points of natural beauty, miniature parks with graveled drives are to be found. The same thing is happening in most states today.

Open Air Shops

Our American habit of rambling over the highways on weekends has converted the borders of our concrete lanes into continuous shops. Here, at a crossroads, you find a farmer's wife tending her roadside market, offering for sale melons, apples, sweet corn, fresh vegetables, strawberries, eggs, poultry and cider.

Drive along a little farther and you see a display of vases, urns, and sundials.

Coast another mile or two and you come upon a small shed bearing the sign "Fishworms, night crawlers, bait."

Farther down the highway, countless weather vanes, carved in the shape of roosters and ships, are stuck in the ground.

As you approach population centers, more pretentious highway shops appear. Here is a drive-in ice cream store, with waitresses to serve you in your car. Beyond is an eat shop, surrounded by a parking lot. Over there is a china shop, farther on a cheese store.

As you approach a golf course, an enterprising salesman offers you linen hats with transparent visors at a dollar a throw. Everywhere over the land ambitious salesmen are displaying their wares along the edges of the concrete to lure your dollar.

We mentioned golf. When you get down to it, golf owes its widespread popularity to the fact that everybody drives a car. It's no accident that the number of golf courses multiplied as car ownership increased. There were only two hundred golf courses in the United States in 1914. Now there are 4,950, public and private.

Between golf, nearby beaches and lakes, state parks, and national parks and monuments, the American public, with a family

car and a moderate budget, has a wealth of riches on which to
draw for weekend and vacation entertainment. This very freedom of selection has made people reluctant to settle on one spot,
buy a summer cottage, and return there year after year.

Travel has become a big business. The American Automobile
Association estimates from Census Bureau figures for 1954 that
vacation touring is a $12 billion business, in which 66 million
people in 22 million cars spend $2 billion for fuel and other car
costs, another $3 billion for lodging, $4 billion on food, and
nearly $3 billion on souvenirs, admissions and amusement. And
this doesn't count what was spent getting ready for the trip.

Travel on this scale is something new on the face of the
earth, and what it means in the breaking down of sectionalism,
appreciation of our country, and breadth of personal viewpoint
our psychologists will have to decide. All we can say is that it
has happened. . . .

The Rich and the Poor Ride

At first thought, you might wonder whether a family man
with an income of less than $2,000 a year could afford to own
an automobile.

Nevertheless he does. A survey made in 1952 shows that
two fifths of all families in this low-income group own cars. In
the $2,000-$3,000 group, two thirds of all families own automobiles and above that income, car-ownership is practically universal.

The casual observer of the American scene might assume
that every family in the country must have a car to get around
in, but in large cities where mass transportation is highly developed, many households do without an automobile. The smaller the city, the more universal is car ownership, and where
homes are somewhat removed from community centers, two-car
families are becoming common. Of all the car-owning families
in the United States, 12 per cent own more than one car, and
many of these two-car families are in the lowest income group.

Plainly enough, in this country, the rich and the poor ride.
It is interesting to seek the reasons why this has happened. . . .

In 1925, the average retail price of all cars was $910.46 (at the factory, including all taxes and standard equipment).

By 1942, it is true that car prices were much higher. The average retail price had risen to $2,168. But wages had risen even more. According to the Bureau of Labor Statistics, weekly earnings of workers in all manufacturing industries had gone up from $24.37 in 1925 to $71.64 in 1954. To buy a car in 1925, a worker had to lay out about 37 weekly pay checks. In 1954, his car cost him about 30 weekly pay checks. In terms of hours, he worked 1,664 hours to own a car in 1925 and 1,198 hours in 1954. . . .

More important in spreading ownership than higher wages is the American system of car purchase. When John Doe wants to buy a new car he doesn't have to dig down into his savings account for the full price. He turns in his used car and receives credit that amounts roughly to a down payment. For the balance he signs twelve to twenty-four monthly notes and drives out of the dealer's place with a new automobile.

Time payments began as early as 1912, the buyer paying something over half down and the balance in one or two installments. As time payments became more general, it became customary to require a down payment of one third and the balance in twelve monthly installments. The exact terms have varied with the times. The net effect of financing and trading-in has been to permit a man to acquire a new car for little or no cash outlay and "painless" payments spread over a period of time. About two thirds of our buyers finance their car purchases this way.

Trading-in cars, a practice that "grew up" with the automobile business, provides the owner with an ideal method of liquidating his present investment. If a man wanted to get rid of his present furniture in order to reequip his house, he'd have to undertake the task of selling his furniture piece by piece, or look up a second-hand dealer and get a price. He could hardly go down to any store and get an "allowance" on his old furniture, to be applied against his new purchase. Yet the automobile dealer provides exactly this service.

The automobile dealer has been in the habit of considering this matter of accepting used cars a "problem." Yet if he didn't offer this convenience he could hardly expect to sell as many cars as he does.

Dealers today not only accept a used car when they sell a new car. When they come to sell the used car, they frequently take an older used car in order to complete the sale. Then they must get rid of this car in turn. . . . The marketing of used cars has steadily increased until it has dwarfed in numbers, if not in dollar volumes, the new car business. Where, in 1919, dealers sold one used car, or less, for every new car, in 1954 the ratio was two used for each new.

Today the man of limited income can buy a wide variety of cars at prices ranging down to a few dollars. Manufacturers who have tried to compete with the used car market by offering a "stripped down" low-cost *new car* have fared badly. During the depression, attempts to sell "standard" models in competition with "de luxes" and "customs" made little headway. Efforts to sell the European-type small car met with little success. People could get a full-size used car for less money.

The automobile may be compared to a package containing approximately 120,000 miles of transportation. The man of low income can't afford to buy the full package, any more than he can afford to lay in ten tons of coal for the winter. He buys whatever part of the package he can afford. If he has enough money he buys the last 90,000 miles. If his cash is extremely limited he may buy only the last 10,000 miles. . . .

Taxing and Regulatory Policy

A final factor in our mass ownership of cars has been our Federal and state taxing and regulatory policies. The American public has been fortunate in that these policies, while not always equitable, have not been unduly restrictive of car use, car design, or car ownership.

Comparisons of taxes paid by Americans and those paid by Europeans are difficult. In general, Americans have been required to pay a smaller part of their real income for the privilege of owning and driving a car than most people living in Europe.

Just as important as this fact, is the fact that taxes in this country haven't been of a kind that unduly hampered the automobile designer. This hasn't been true in foreign countries. . . .

There are other reasons for wide car ownership in the United States. We are blessed, in this country, with an ample supply of low-cost fuel. Wage scales in the United States are far higher than those in other countries. Furthermore, people in the United States have always had confidence in the future, and therefore have been willing to spend their money. The very size of the nation, affording a large market without artificial trade barriers, has been a factor in mass ownership, because the size of the market has permitted large-scale manufacture, and this in turn has permitted the kind of tooling and productive processes that have enabled the American automobile manufacturer to make high-value cars at relatively low cost. . . .

We spend about ten per cent of our national income on automobile transportation. Department of Commerce figures for 1954 show that we spent almost $24 billion on automobiles, as compared to a national income of $300 billion. If we were to say that the average American family spends ten dollars out of every hundred on his car, we wouldn't be far off. And if we eliminate the 25 per cent of all families that do not own a car, the rest of us actually spend more than ten out of every hundred on our automobiles.

The wisdom or unwisdom of devoting this much money to the car is a subject that is beyond the scope of this report. The data are presented as a matter of simple fact. This is what the people have done. It is the way they have wanted to spend their money.

Today it is second-nature for all Americans, upon leaving the house, the factory, or the office, to climb in behind the wheel of an automobile. This little act has become the great American habit. The purpose may be only to drive down to the corner drug store. It may be to visit Mexico City or Yellowstone Park. It may be to sell hairpins or radios or fishing tackle to jobbers over a thousand-mile sales route.

All these combined errands, multiplied millions of times every day, have changed the nature of our countryside, our cities, and our government, and our pattern of daily life. The United States of today is far different from the United States of 1919. Today, we take for granted that part of our heritage is to possess our own personal means of transport, so that we can come and go, whenever and wherever we please, within the limits of our free time and our pocketbooks. This concept of freedom of transport is the very essence of the revolution which has made the car a vital part of our lives.

We're a car-traveling people.

PAYING FOR OUR ROADS [5]

A hundred years ago, whatever work was done on the roads was a local affair. The counties and towns tried to collect road taxes from property owners, but only the rich could pay. Most farmers had little hard cash, so they "worked out" their taxes by laboring on the roads occasionally. As years passed by and economic conditions improved, people were able to pay in money instead of labor; but the local property tax was still the only source of funds for highways.

Then the states began to provide aid to the counties, and later to take control of the main roads. The money for this highway work came from the state general funds, which were largely the receipts of property taxes. . . . Today, the property tax provides a little more than one half of the money spent for roads by the county and local governments. But for the states, the coming of the automobile made a great change in state highway financing. The motor vehicle brought a need for great improvement of the highways, and at the same time provided a new source of taxes.

Taxes on the Highway User

New York, in 1901, was the first state to require registration of motor vehicles. In the beginning this licensing was a means

[5] From *Highways in the United States,* pamphlet. United States Department of Commerce. Bureau of Public Roads. Washington 25, D.C. 1954. p8-12.

of regulating the vehicles. It was soon recognized by New York and other states as also being a good way to collect taxes for highways from the people who used them. . . . By 1917 every state had a motor-vehicle registration law. Special taxes on trucks and buses, driver licenses, and title, transfer, and inspection fees soon followed in most states. . . .

In 1919, Oregon started to collect a 1-cent-per-gallon tax on gasoline, to provide funds for highways, and within ten years every state had adopted the gasoline tax. . . . The gasoline tax is extremely successful because it costs the motorist only a few cents at a time, yet it brings in enormous amounts of money in total. Too, it taxes the motor-vehicle operator directly in accordance with his use of the highways. State gasoline taxes now range from 3 cents to 7 cents a gallon. The average for the country is 4.8 cents.

The Federal Government collects a gasoline tax of 2 cents per gallon [increased to 3 cents in 1956] and also taxes lubricating oil, new motor vehicles and parts, and tires and tubes, But these are taxes for the general support of the Government, as are the Federal taxes on such varied things as telephone service, train tickets, and television sets. The money from the automotive taxes goes into the United States Treasury, and bears no relation to the Federal aid provided for highways.

Highway-user taxes are not limited entirely to the states, although many states forbid their use by local units. Local motor-vehicle registration taxes are collected in about fifteen states, mostly by the cities. Gasoline taxes are collected by counties or local governments in less than ten states. . . .

The Size of Highway Income

The income for highway purposes collected by the local governments reached a peak over twenty years ago. The high point for cities was $787 million in 1930. For counties and townships it was $550 million in 1928. During the depression the yield from property taxes dropped sharply, reaching a low in 1934 of about $600 million for the local rural and urban units combined. Since then it has gradually increased, interrupted only by World War II. In 1952, the local property tax produced $1.1 billion, of which 43 per cent was collected by the rural governments and 57 per cent by the cities.

Money used for highways from the state general funds has been less each year, as income from highway-user taxes has grown. In 1952, $25 million (net) was provided for highways from state general funds. The states collected $128 million from road-users in 1921. In 1952, this source produced over $3 billion. Of this total gasoline taxes yielded $1.968 billion; vehicle registrations and fees, $1.07 billion; and special truck and bus fees, $64 million. Not all of this was spent for state highways, however, for the cost of collecting the road-user taxes was $120 million. The local governments were given $819 million for their roads and streets. And $203 million went for nonhighway purposes. There has been a trend over the years to stop this flow of road-user taxes to nonhighway uses, and twenty-four states now have laws forbidding it. . . .

One thing must be remembered, in considering the size of our current income for highways. The total income is larger than ever before. Highway-user tax rates have advanced slowly— the average state gasoline tax has increased 21 per cent since 1941—but there are far more vehicles paying these taxes. However, the costs of construction and maintenance have more than doubled during the same period. Consequently, funds available in 1952 bought less highway work than the money available in 1941. Yet the need is far greater, for there are 18 million more vehicles on the road now, and the number is constantly growing.

Federal Aid for Highways

Congress provided $5 million to the states for highways in 1917, the first year of the Federal-aid program. In the following year the amount was $10 million. During the next twelve years the rate was about $75 million a year. In 1931-33 and 1936-37 the annual rate was increased to $125 million. It jumped to $200 million a year in 1938-39, and then dropped to an average of $142 million a year during the following four years.

In the depression years the regular Federal aid was added to (and replaced in 1934 and 1935) by special public works funds which were intended to provide extensive highway improvements and at the same time give jobs to millions of people who were out of work. A total of $1.2 billion was thus provided between 1930 and 1935. Work done by the Work Projects Administration is not included in this total. Normal Federal-aid work was stopped late in 1941, at the beginning of World War II. . . .

In 1946 the regular Federal-aid program was resumed, on a scale larger than ever before. For 1946-48, $500 million a year was provided, and in each of the years 1950 and 1951, $450 million. For 1952 and 1953, $500 million a year has been made available, and for 1954 and 1955, $575 million.

Borrowing for Road Building

In the early years of modern road building, many counties and cities borrowed money to pay for highway construction. They still do. Massachusetts, in 1893, was the first state to borrow for highways, and other states soon followed. The growth of the motor vehicle was so fast that current income at that time could not build enough roads and bridges for them.

But the states could foresee that highway-user taxes would yield a huge annual income in the future. So they issued highway bonds, and arranged for the money so borrowed to be paid off in later years from road-user taxes. Some states had laws forbidding them to issue bonds, but they made use of the borrowing power of their counties and townships.

The process still continues. Each year some debts are being paid off, and new money is being borrowed. In 1940 the total state highway debt (including toll facility obligations) was $1.896 billion, that of the counties and townships was $1.29 billion, and that of the cities was $1.45 billion. During the war years borrowing was less, but since the beginning of 1947 bonds issued for highways have exceeded redemptions. At the end of 1952, total public highway debt had reached a new high of $5.839 billion.

Our Investment in Highways

It is fairly obvious that even though a highway or street is regularly maintained, eventually it will wear out. To emphasize the point, certain questions may be asked. How much has been invested in our highway plant? How much of the original investment remains? What is the average age and service life of the remaining value of the original investment?

It was estimated that $75.5 billion (January 1953 price level) were spent for the construction of highways and streets in the United States during the period, 1914-52. Of the improvements made, a portion costing $60.7 billion remained in service at the beginning of 1953. The difference of $14.8 billion represents investment that was lost through road abandonment or was not salvaged for further use in the reconstruction of a road or street. Of the roads costing $60.7 billion still in service, many have aged and a substantial portion of the probable total life has been consumed. In other words, the original investment has depreciated to a much lesser figure. The depreciated investment was estimated to be $36.9 billion at the beginning of 1953, or less than one-half of the original investment of $75.5 billion.

Of the original improvements still remaining in service, it was estimated that their average age was 14.6 years, and that the average remaining service life was 28.2 years.

What do such statistics about our highways tell us? They give us an indication as to whether we are building highways faster than they wear out. In the years before World War II, we were gaining in providing highway facilities, but during the war the trend was reversed. In the postwar period, the volume of capital outlay again exceeded the rate of obsolescence, but it took until the beginning of 1953 for the depreciated investment to recover to the level reached in 1941.

A comparison made of the amount of depreciated investment in highways per vehicle registered shows that at the end of 1941 the amount was $1,064, and at the beginning of 1953, the figure had dropped to $691.

Road Taxes and the Individual Vehicle

The total collections from highway-user taxes seem astronomically large. But how do they affect the individual motor-vehicle owner? As would be expected, the big truck-trailers pay much more than automobiles. There is a wide variation in the fees charged by different states. And in twenty-two states, farmers' trucks are registered for much less than the regular rate.

For a light passenger car, the average registration fee is less than $12 and the state gasoline tax costs its operator $30 a year. For a five-axle truck-tractor and semitrailer combination the registration and other related fees total $1,148, and state motor-fuel taxes average $955 a year. It is interesting to see the effect of type of operation on road-user taxes. The average registration fee for a stake truck owned by a farmer is $31; for the same truck operated by a private business the registration costs $51; and for the same truck used in contract hauling it costs $94. Because of the differences in their annual travel, the state gasoline tax for the farm truck would be $29 a year; for the privately owned truck, $70; and for the contract truck, $117.

In addition to these taxes, many states have a personal-property tax on motor vehicles. The average property tax ranges from $28 a year for a light automobile to $413 for a five-axle tractor-semitrailer. All vehicles, of course, pay the Federal gasoline tax. Common carrier trucks, hauling on a fixed route for anyone who wants freight service, pay various special fees which often are quite large. Some are business levies rather than highway-user taxes.

Taxes and Total Operating Costs

Let us see how taxes are related to total costs of owning and operating a typical passenger car. Over a period of ten years, the total costs would average $755 a year, of which $674 is for the cost of buying the car, upkeep and repair, gasoline and oil, tires, insurance, etc. The highway-user taxes—state gasoline tax and registration fee—amount to $43 a year. Of the remainder, $9 is for title fee and property tax, $14 for Federal gasoline and oil tax, and $15 for Federal excise taxes on the passenger car (when it was bought new), parts, and tires.

Expressed in a simpler way, for every dollar of expense, the gasoline tax took 6 cents and all other taxes 4 cents. Of the other 90 cents, 21 cents is accounted for in the cost of buying the car, 18 cents for gasoline (not counting taxes), 19 cents for upkeep and repair, 12 cents for garage and parking, 14 cents for insurance, and 6 cents for oil, tires, and accessories.

In terms of travel, it costs 7.5 cents a mile to own and operate this typical car (including depreciation). Of this amount, one third of one cent is for the state gasoline tax and one tenth of one cent for the state registration fee.

II. THE TURNING WHEELS

EDITOR'S INTRODUCTION

On September 20, 1893, a twenty-three-year-old toolmaker named J. Frank Duryea engaged the rubber and leather transmission on his mechanized phaeton buggy and drove it slowly up Spruce Street in Springfield, Massachusetts, and down Florence. There, overcome by the experience of building and operating the first automobile in the United States—and doubting its friction transmission would get it back to the shop—he pulled over to the sidewalk and encouraged his four-cycle, water-cooled engine to a gasping halt. Then he stepped to the ground and into history as father of the greatest social, economic, and industrial revolution ever to sweep America.

The extent of that revolution is evident in every article that follows. In the first the editors of *Business Week* describe some of the changes that can be wrought in our communities merely by the opening of a new road and indicate that this revolution, despite valiant rear guard actions by adherents of the status quo, has scarcely begun. Other articles bear out this contention, but many show that change is not necessarily desirable *per se* and that in many respects we have not lived up to its challenge. This is especially true of our laws, notoriously hobbled to precedent and the past, for we have allowed over 60 million deadly weapons to wander our roads under a jumble of state laws that vie with one another in absurdity and unreason. The chaos and inadequacy of our judicial procedures are pointed out by Judge Hofstadter in "Our Laggard Liability Laws," together witht suggestions for a far-reaching reform, and the need and method of refurbishment are discussed by the editor of *Collier's* in "Forty-eight Ways to Get One Ticket" and by J. Edward Johnston in "Fast Roads and Slow Traffic."

Other writers suggest that we are a nation on wheels that might be spinning too fast for our own good. John L. Springer and George Koether—in "Collecting Tolls with Both Hands" and "Tax Road or Toll Road?"—discuss the two principal methods of highway financing, but *Business Week*, in "Bumpy Going for the Toll Roads," advances the possibility that this continuing controversy will eventually be settled in Wall Street and the toll booths rather than in Washington or the state legislatures. And, while John S. Worley argues "The Case for Trucks" against David G. Wittels, David Cort wonders, in "Our Strangling Highways," if we are not likely to be smothered in the ever-expanding web of concrete that brought the trucks into being. Many viewpoints are expressed on the use and misuse of our highways, but none deviates from the belief that our state and national governments—like J. Frank Duryea when he replaced his original free-piston motor with an engine based on "sound and well-tried principles"—will have the wit and ingenuity to discard the evils of the automotive revolution without retarding its progress and will build a network of roads that will enrich us in peace and defend us in war.

HIGHWAYS BRING CHANGE [1]

On a bright, sunny morning last week, Mr. Oliver Stockwell, salesman, resident of Providence and owner of a 1954 Buick, backed out of his driveway, wove his way to U S Route 1, and headed north for Portland, Maine.

Since this was New England, and since in New England "all roads lead to Boston," Route 1 eventually took Stockwell to that city—or would have had he stayed on it. But some fifteen miles south of Boston, he deserted the highway, cut out to the west, and proceeded to make an end run around the city's outskirts. About fifty minutes later, having completed a rough semicircle around Boston, Stockwell was back on Route 1 pointed toward Portland, with Boston behind him.

This automotive sidestep—which put more miles on Stockwell's speedometer but took innumerable points off his blood

[1] From "New England Highway Upsets Old Way of Life." *Business Week.* p 186-8. May 14, 1955. Reprinted by special permission from *Business Week*, a McGraw-Hill publication. Copyright 1955 by McGraw-Hill Publishing Company.

pressure by saving him from Boston's traffic congestion—was made possible by a new, still unfinished highway that is already one of the most famous in the East. Referred to somewhat grandly as the Boston Circumferential Highway, most people know it simply as Route 128.

However it is labeled, though, there is no doubt as to its reputation: In the last two years, it has become a classic example of how a new road can change the traffic pattern of a metropolitan area—and completely remake the face of the landscape around it.

The new Route 128, when it is finished, will curve around Boston for some eighty miles, linking the old fishing port of Gloucester on the northeast with the Hull-Cohasset recreation area on the southeast. A divided, six-lane, limited-access expressway, it forms an outer loop for much of its course along the old Route 128, a two-lane blacktop with a cowpath heritage.

As far back as 1936, the Massachusetts Department of Public Works began the job of remaking Route 128. . . . But by 1947, very little had been done on the new road; the skimpiness of prewar appropriations, and the total clampdown on spending during the war years, combined to put only eight new miles of the highway on the map.

From 1947 on, though, the tempo picked up. With a master plan for state roads—and the wherewithal from three bond issues and general appropriations—nearly sixty miles, starting from the northeast end of the eventual eighty-mile semicircle, were complete or under construction by last week [1955]. . . .

These miles since 1947 have brought the changes. And a driver has only to cruise the southern leg of 128 to see how tremendous some of the changes have been.

Expressways, the American Society of Planning Officials has said, may make cities of us all. What the new Route 128 has done is simply what other expressways have done—create demand for industrial and commercial land near the super-road, open a new market for residential property in the towns close by. The difference is that 128 has done it with a vengeance, though whether from fad or legitimate trend no one yet knows.

Since 1951, more than forty new buildings have been started or finished on what was once farm or vacant land along the path of the new road (the exact total depends on how far off the route you stray to count).

All this building—and a conservative estimate of plant costs so far would be about $100 million—has left its economic, as well as physical, mark on the landscape. What the Westchester County Department of Planning found in a three-year study of the effects of parkways in New York—namely that the price of land along the parkway jumped more than in other parts of the community—shows up even more dramatically along 128.

Land that brought $50 to $100 an acre before the highway went through, commands $5,000 to $10,000 an acre today, if it rates as a first-class industrial site. In Dedham, for instance, a twenty-eight-acre tract that was bought for $300 an acre in 1934 was sold to R. M. Bradley & Company, a Boston real estate firm, for $220,000 last year.

These effects of Route 128—the building it has brought on, the land inflation—are obvious to even a casual observer. What is not so apparent, though, is the impact the highway has had on Boston itself and on the towns along the route.

For Boston, the "magic semicircle" has meant less congestion, but also a loss of industry. Many of 128's new plants—and all fall in the "desirable" class of light manufacturing, warehousing, and office—are refugees from the cramp and crowd of central Boston. For the towns, the highway and the plants have admittedly meant more tax revenue. But plants—and more people—are not unmixed blessing, for they change a town and run up its bill for services. . . .

1. A "Bedroom" Changes

Dedham is a pleasant, middle-class town of 21,500 people, the county seat of Norfolk County, and for years one of Boston's bedrooms. Settled in 1636—early residents were screened to see that they met standards of "sobriety and industry"—it is as old as Harvard College and has at least one landmark, the oldest frame house in America, to prove it.

In the Dedham area, the southern leg of Route 128 is still under construction. But because of the road, Dedham began to change as far back as 1953.

There has always been a little industry in Dedham. Boston Envelope Company is there and years ago—before the turn of the century—a carpet mill and a textile mill flourished in its midst. The town, though, made no special effort to bring in more plants and, indeed, saw little reason for having them. Its Boston commuters were satisfied with Dedham as it was—residential, small-townish, a good place to raise a family. At least they were, until tax rates changed their minds.

Between 1949 and 1953, Dedham's tax rate edged up from $42 per $1,000 of assessed valuation to $49.60. Faced with a continuing population increase—the actual jump between 1950 and 1954 was 3,500 people—and the need for still more schools and services, there seemed nothing in sight but further hikes. This, and the coming of the new Route 128, finally brought the people of Dedham, at town meeting in 1953, to pass a resolution setting up a seven-man industrial commission. Under the chairmanship of Town Accountant John J. Flynn, the commission was to see if it could now get selected light industry into the areas that had been zoned for it in the 1920's.

How much of what happened after that can be chalked up to the lure of Route 128, and how much reflects the work of the commission, there is no saying. Nevertheless, by the town meeting of 1955, Dedham had its industry, not in the old zones, to be sure, but in land specifically rezoned for it.

All told [as of May 1955], three plants are finished, or are almost so, and a fourth is waiting to start. General Motors Corporation moved into its new $350,000 training center for New England mechanics last year. Fabric Research Laboratories, Inc., which built on land adjacent to the GM center, expects to open its $250,000 building sometime next month. In July, Rust Craft Greeting Cards, which like Fabric Research came out from Boston, figures to get into a $3 million plant that it broke ground on last spring. Still to come is a $1.8 million plant that Allied Container Corporation plans to build on part of a twenty-eight-acre tract that was once a gravel pit.

Aside from these industrial settlers, Dedham has had some commercial callers come to stay since the highway began running past its door. Stop 'n' Shop has started work on a new 15,000-square-foot supermarket; First National Stores plans another of about the same size; and New England Bell Telephone has bought up land for a new two-story exchange building. . . .

How has all this changed Dedham? Physically, the new buildings have made a difference, of course. But it would be hard to say they have started remaking Dedham's face. The buildings themselves are unobtrusive, more institutional in look than anything else. They blend, rather than contrast, with the rest of the town's façade.

Where the difference shows—or more properly will show—is in the tax rolls.

Using a rule-of-thumb assessment at 55 per cent of appraised value, Dedham figures that its four plants and the new telephone building will add about $140,000 a year to town coffers. Based on the experience of other towns, Dedham believes this revenue will far out-distance the cost of the services it will have to provide to the companies. Thus it hopes, perhaps optimistically, that it will be able to go ahead on some of its badly needed schools and other facilities—and still hold the line on the tax rate (last year's rate dipped $1 to $48.60).

The fact is, though, that Dedham has already had to foot a sizable bill for services just to get the companies in and ready to operate. The town land it sold to Rust Craft had been bought for $65,000 in 1948, for a cemetery. Rust Craft paid $162,000 for the tract. But the town had to build a road into the plant that will cost it about $145,000. In the case of General Motors —where it sold three acres that had been town infirmary land for $50,000—it had to take part of the price to extend its sewerage.

At this point, real estate men say it is too early to spot any uptrend in residential property values that can be attributed directly to the new highway. Actually, town officials see no marked influx of people from either the road or the plants. Partly, they base this on the belief that the labor market that plants will draw on is already outside of Boston and will see no reason to shift to Dedham.

Some people feel, though, that all this may be whistling in the dark, that Dedham is bound to continue gaining population, and that the new highway and plants are simply accelerators. If this is true, Dedham may face the same tax problems ten years from now that it did in 1953.

2. *An Industrial City Grows*

Waltham sits beside the Charles River, practically due west of Boston, and looks for all the world like what it is: a New England industrial city that has been industrial as far back as anyone can remember.

A city of almost 50,000 people today, Waltham had a paper mill as long ago as 1788. Through the 1800's, though, its name came to mean watches and textiles, and the clock on Main Street still proclaims it as "The Watch City." Today with close to two hundred companies in manufacturing, warehousing, and service, Waltham prefers to think of itself as "The Precision City." In its industrial complex, watches are only a small tick now.

The new Route 128 pushed past Waltham, on its western outskirts, and was open to traffic in late 1951. Waltham saw in the highway a chance to lure a selection of new industry—especially non-nuisance manufacturing—and it responded in 1952 by rezoning for limited commercial development four hundred acres that had been set aside for residential building.

So far, Waltham can count six new plants on what was once the farm land—and piggeries—that stretched along its western rim. The biggest project, potentially, is the 110-acre industrial center that Cabot, Cabot & Forbes, the Boston realtor, is developing . . . Sylvania Electric Products, Inc., is already partly in a 120,000-square-foot plant that it has taken in the center under long-term lease from Cabot, Cabot & Forbes.

Polaroid Corporation, which has built one plant off the highway at Waltham, now talks of putting up three more. Tracerlab, Inc., has a $1.8 million plant under construction, and Vectron, Inc., a Waltham-based machine-working company, is going ahead on a $500,000 building. On the brow overlooking Cambridge Reservoir, Boston Manufacturers Mutual Fire Insurance Company has a $1.5 million structure under way. Taken together, all this means somewhere in the neighborhood of $5 million worth of new plants for Waltham's tax books. In terms of revenue, figured on a 50 per cent assessment ratio, the annual take would run to about $128,000. . . .

The gravy portion of this, however, is not nearly so big as it looks. Partly because of the new plants along 128, the city has had to embark on a $1.3 million trunk sewerage program. Water supply has had to be bolstered, and pressure stepped up. About $70,000 is going into new mains and a 1 million gallon standpipe.

Route 128, with its limited access, means more congestion, too, even though it may be a concentrated congestion confined to one or two city streets. City Engineer Herbert Howe believes that Waltham will probably have to face up to widening and improving the main feeder roads leading to the highway. Howe thinks police and fire forces may have to be increased some, too.

Like Dedham, though, Waltham believes that the services it has to offer new industry cost most in the first few years. After that, the tax revenues top the new costs. In any event, it sees nothing like the continuing $250 loss it takes each year on a $15,000 house. The city figures the services it provides come out to about $600 per residence, and the most it gets back from, say, a $15,000 house is about $350 taxes.

At this point, it seems doubtful that Waltham will have a strong residential boom because of the new highway—though it may feel added pressure for existing space. The city was built up long ago. Most of its desirable sites have been well worked over.

3. An Historic Town Resists

For Lexington, Route 128 has either made things better or made things worse. The verdict depends on just how one feels about Lexington.

Lexington is a town that has grown by spurts—one in the early 1900's, another in the middle 1920's, and a tremendous one in the postwar period. Between 1940 and 1950, while Boston's population remained relatively static, Lexington's shot up by 31.5 per cent. Since 1950, it has climbed another 5,000—from 17,000 to 22,000.

For a town that wanted to grow, this would be all to the good. But the fact is that Lexington—or at least a good part of its people—would rather not grow at all. They prefer Lexington as it is, or was. And in this sense, Route 128 simply upsets things more.

The town where the Minute Man still stands upon the village green, and where the first battle of the Revolutionary War was fought, has so far managed to survive most of the uglier on-slaughts of the twentieth century. Along its streets—Lexington is 90 per cent single-family houses—the feeling is still one of a small country town. The houses are good, mainly upper-middle class in the $12,000 to $20,000 bracket, with some pushing up to $40,000. There is not enough industry to talk about.

What Route 128 has done for Lexington is give it an adequate link with the other towns on the rim and a tie to the radial routes. What it has done, too, is to make it all the more attractive for people to choose it for their bedroom.

Lexington's defense against being overrun has been to tighten its zoning requirements. But despite this—as the population figures show—it has not yet been able to stunt its growth.

And the inevitable result has been, of course, a need for more and more city services—requiring more and more money to satisfy. Although Lexington's tax rate has not jumped spectac-ularly . . . the drain has shown up in the town's bonded debt. Where it owed only $822,000 in 1948, its debt last year had climbed to $4.5 million. Meanwhile, assessments had gone up from $27 million to $45 million.

Realization that revenue and spending will at some point have to be brought into balance has convinced some of the people of Lexington that it could do with a little of the sort of industry that has been going up in other towns along Route 128. Actu-ally, Lexington has some six hundred acres that are already zoned for light industry along the highway. But so far nothing has been built on them.

Two years ago a proposal was made to double the zone to fit in with some development plans. The town meeting voted it down. Again last year, a bid was made to add a forty-acre slice; town meeting voted it down again. This spring the town finally approved, by a voice vote, the rezoning of eleven acres that were tied to a proposal to build a plastics plant. . . .

At this point, there is no telling when and if new industry will come into Lexington. But there are signs that the opposition to it is weakening. The most potent argument working against the opponents is the dollar-and-cents one—the fact that the town has to find new revenue some place.

AND HIGHWAYS BRING DEATH [2]

Accidents on the highways, in fifty-five years, have killed more Americans than all United States wars since 1775. Eight wars, over a period of 180 years, cost 1,130,393 American lives. Since 1900, deaths on the highway have totaled 1,149,414.

Highway deaths in 1955 alone numbered 38,500, the highest in fourteen years. This rising total is leading to demands for better roads, for more control of speed, for building greater safety into cars and for stiffer penalties for traffic-law violations. . . .

The Revolutionary War lasted eight years—from 1775 to 1783—and cost 4,435 American lives. Motor vehicles last year killed more than that many every forty-three days.

[The] War of 1812 lasted until 1815, with 2,260 United States deaths. [The] Mexican War, waged in 1846-48, cost 13,283 American lives. Deaths in both those wars were equaled on United States roads in just five months of 1955.

In the Civil War, 1861-65, a total of 529,332 lost their lives, more than half of them dying of disease. But more people died in accidents on United States roads in the sixteen years ending with 1955.

[2] From "Highway Deaths Are Rising." *U. S. News & World Report.* 40:50-1. February 3, 1956. Reprinted from *U. S. News & World Report*, an independent weekly news magazine published at Washington. Copyright 1956 United States News Publishing Company.

The brief Spanish-American War cost 2,446 United States lives. World War I deaths reached 116,563, and World War II brought 407,828 American deaths. In recent years, 54,246 Americans died in Korea. Yet the toll of autos has topped the loss of lives in all these wars.

When it comes to injuries, motor accidents outstrip the bloodiest war. In 1955, there were more persons injured on United States highways than were wounded on all the battle-fields of the nation's history.

Wounded in action, in eight wars, were 1,276,520 Americans. Highway accidents injured an estimated 1,350,000 in 1955 alone. Since 1900, more than 39 million persons have been injured in motor-vehicle accidents in this country.

Driving is not as dangerous as going to war, but the difference is smaller than might be supposed. In the Korean War, for instance, a youth who spent one year at the front, in combat, would have had one chance in seven of being wounded; one chance in twenty-six of being killed. Actually, American GI's were not kept at the front for a year at a stretch, so their chances were better than these hypothetical odds would indicate.

The American motorist who drives for one year on today's highways has about one chance in fifty of being involved in an accident in which someone is killed or injured. And those who survive the hazards do not become eligible for schooling, loan or medical benefits, as under a GI Bill of Rights.

AUTO ACCIDENTS: CAUSES, CURES [3]

Are traffic accidents getting worse? It depends on how you look at it. The *rate*—number of deaths per 100 million vehicle miles traveled—has gone steadily downward. . . . The annual *number* of deaths reached a peak of 39,969 in 1941. Since World War II this number has fluctuated, with an actual decrease in 1954, but an alarming increase of 10 to 12 per cent during the summer and fall months of 1955. If this continues, the current year's death toll may approach or even equal the 1941 peak.

[3] From an article by Sidney J. Williams, late assistant to the president of the National Safety Council. New York *Times Magazine.* p 15. December 18, 1955. Reprinted by permission.

And don't overlook the injuries—1.25 million each year, of which 100,000 involve the loss of an arm, leg or eye, or other permanent disability. The economic waste comes to more than $4 billion annually.

What is the cause of all this trouble? What is the remedy? Many a layman has a pat answer. The traffic professional knows, alas, that it is not so simple.

Take this not unusual example. A driver who has had several drinks is hurrying homeward on a rainy night. The street is poorly lighted. Suddenly he sees a man crossing ahead of him, his head under an umbrella, and jams on his brakes (which are out of adjustment), skidding into the pedestrian. The cause?

Speed? "I was only going 30."

Alcohol? "I only had four beers."

Brakes? "They were checked just a few months ago."

Pedestrian carelessness? Legally, he had the right of way.

Slippery pavement? Poor lighting? The voters had turned down a bond issue for repaving and better illumination.

The safety man knows that there is no one cause for such an accident. He is interested in going after all the causes, realizing full well that none can be completely done away with.

Police and traffic reports indicate that nearly two thirds of the drivers involved in fatal accidents were violating the law, often on several counts. Nearly half of them were accused of "exceeding speed limit" or "exceeding safe speed." The latter phrase tells more than the former, for speed limits, though necessary, are not an infallible guide to safety. Driving at sixty or even seventy on a straight, level, uncrowded highway may be less dangerous than doing thirty on a narrow, winding, mountain road. The best gauge, stressed more and more by safety workers today, is the degree of *hurry:* impatience to get there a little sooner.

A potent contributing factor is liquor. One out of every ten violators involved in fatal accidents was under the influence of alcohol. Others, according to the reports, "did not have right of way" or "failed to keep right of center line" or passed improperly or disregarded stoplights and signs. Some were driving cars with faulty brakes, tires, lights or other defects.

But all these were circumstances, rather than basic causes. Why do people do these things—drive too fast, drive after drinking, drive in ways which they know, or should know, are illegal and dangerous?

Some—no one knows just how many—are physically or mentally unable to cope with modern traffic. Their vision is too poor, their wits too dull, their reactions too slow—either permanently, or temporarily from fatigue, illness, alcohol. A greater number just don't know how to drive. They were never taught and they have not succeeded in teaching themselves. Still others have enough sense and skill but don't always use them. They are inattentive, careless, reckless. They take chances. They neglect their cars. They think accidents happen only to other people.

The remedies for the traffic toll are as many and varied as the causes. Traffic specialists group them under three familiar E's—Engineering, Education and Enforcement. Any one of the E's, applied intelligently and persistently, will reduce accidents. But what really does the trick is the combination of all of them, through the united efforts of legislative and administrative officials, educators, publicists, and state and city safety organizations.

Here are the main factors involved in a traffic safety program:

The Law. There is abundant proof that strict enforcement by highway police, backed by public education can cut accidents sharply and quickly. Every state now has a driver license law, but only a few states give adequate attention to drivers already licensed. These states keep a central record of each driver's accidents and convictions and, if the record gets bad enough, call him in for an interview and warn him or suspend his license, as the case may require.

The Road. A moron, or any driver who becomes just a bit too careless, can get into trouble on even the best highway. But a road with built-in safety features prevents certain types of accidents and makes safe driving easier. The mileage death rate on expressways or limited access ways of the best modern type is only a quarter to a half as great as on ordinary roads. Even such minor improvements as the widening of narrow pavements, bridges and shoulders bring a marked reduction in accidents.

The School. A number of states and cities hold annual teenage conferences at which several hundred boys and girls, representing their respective schools, meet to talk about traffic and safety. One thing teen-agers always urge is more driver training in high schools. Young drivers who have had such training have only about half as many accidents and violations as those who have not.

The Car. Today's motor vehicle is much safer than its predecessor of ten, let alone twenty or thirty, years ago. But it can still get out of order. Annual or semiannual car tests—compulsory, at official stations, or voluntary, in car check campaigns —should be used in more states and cities. Like better highways, better cars make things easier for the safe driver. But they can't keep the reckless out of trouble.

Governors, mayors and their department heads are the shock troops in the war against accidents. But in a democracy no official can go very far, or last very long, without the support of the people who must obey the laws and pay the taxes—and who vote. A traffic judge said, "If I am trying some prominent citizen for drunk driving I get twenty phone calls urging me to go easy on him. I wish even ten people would call up to promise support if I put him in jail."

Organization at the national, state and especially at the community level is the greatest need. Officials and civic groups must get together and agree on traffic safety measures which the officials will put into effect and the newspapers and citizens will support.

AUTO ACCIDENTS AND INSURANCE [4]

Traffic accidents cost 38,300 lives in the United States during 1953 and resulted in injuries to more than 1.33 million persons. The total economic loss . . . was nearly $4 billion of which $1.66

[4] From *Automobile Liability Insurance,* by Helen B. Shaffer, author and economist. *Editorial Research Reports.* 1, no 12:225-36. March 23, 1954. Reprinted by permission.

billion represented property damage. Although the accident rate, in proportion to miles driven, has declined in most states during recent years, the actual number of traffic accidents has shown a steady increase. The growing demand for effective financial responsibility laws reflects public recognition that a certain amount of death and destruction on the highways is inevitable, under even the best safety codes, and that ways must be found to assure compensation to the accident victims.

Until World War I, serious automobile accidents were so few that traffic fatalities were not recorded separately by the Bureau of Vital Statistics. By 1917, however, there were upward of 10,000 traffic deaths and state legislatures began to consider special measures to assure financial protection to the victims or their survivors. The usual legal award of damages had already proved futile in the many cases in which the motorist involved lacked sufficient funds to pay the amount assessed.

The one test of compulsory liability insurance has so far been provided by the 1925 Massachusetts law [New York's Compulsory Liability Insurance Law went into effect January 1, 1957]. . . . Under this statute no motor vehicle may be registered in the state unless the application is accompanied by a certificate showing that the owner has provided for payment of valid personal injury claims arising out of his negligence. The required security may take the form of an insurance policy covering at least $5,000 for injury or death to one person and $10,000 if there is more than one victim of a single accident, or it may be a surety bond or cash deposit. The insurance must cover not only the owner but any other person allowed to drive his car.

The Massachusetts state insurance commissioner has authority to fix rates on policies and surety bonds. He establishes insurance rates annually, after hearings at which insurance carriers customarily file data for the previous year relating to adequacy of premium rates. Decisions of the commissioner may be challenged in the courts. As a further protection for the motorist, a board of appeals passes on whether an insurance company is justified in refusing to issue or renew a policy thus withholding from insurance underwriters the power to determine arbitrarily who should drive an automobile in the state.

Experience under the Massachusetts law has shown serious gaps in the coverage required. Compulsory provisions do not include liability for property damage, and the required bodily injury insurance applies only to accidents occurring on public streets and highways within the state. To be fully protected, the Massachusetts motorist must take out additional insurance against property damage; personal injury from accidents in alleys, parking areas, garages, private driveways, and repair shops; injuries to guests in his car; and deaths or injuries resulting from accidents in other states.

It is contended that the $5,000/$10,000 minimum set by law tends to become the maximum purchased by the motorist in Massachusetts and is too low to cover some types of claims. No protection is afforded victims of accidents caused by hit-and-run drivers, by insurance dodgers, by uninsured drivers from other states, by unauthorized or stolen-car drivers.

A pioneering law enacted by the Connecticut legislature in 1925 required a show of financial responsibility for future accidents by any motorist who failed to satisfy a judgment after thirty days or who was convicted of reckless driving, driving while intoxicated, or leaving the scene of an accident. The American Automobile Association followed the general lines of this law when it first drafted a model law in 1928 and other states soon fell in line. Such financial responsibility laws proved less effective than their framers had anticipated, because they permitted the accident-prone driver to continue as a road hazard until a conviction or until a judgment had been obtained against him and remained unsatisfied. Damage claims were rarely entered against drivers known to be without financial resources. Thus, instead of limiting all motorists to "one bite," the laws allowed some motorists several accidents before being required to show financial responsibility.

In 1937, New Hampshire added to its financial responsibility law, a so-called "security" feature. It provided that the state vehicle department, on receipt of an accident report, should determine the amount of security sufficient in its judgment to satisfy any potential awards, and required all uninsured drivers involved to post security or forfeit their driving privileges. Within a few years, a half dozen states had accepted the New Hampshire pattern. . . . Forty-four states now have laws of the safety responsibility type.

Much of the support for stronger liability insurance laws is due to the number of accident victims who, because of loopholes in the present statutes, are not able to collect damage awards. Following the lead of eight Canadian provinces, two American states—New Jersey and North Dakota—have set up "unsatisfied judgment" funds to meet this particular problem and other states are studying their operation. Under this system, a fund to cover unsatisfied judgments is built up by additional fees collected from all motorists at the time of annual registration. Awards from the fund are made only when the claimant has exhausted all other legal methods of obtaining compensation. . . .

The unsatisfied judgment plan is criticized as a violation of the risk-sharing principles of insurance and an unfair imposition on responsible motorists. . . . The Safety Responsibility Committee of the AAA rejected a proposal that an unsatisfied judgment plan be incorporated in its safety responsibility law. The reasons given were that existence of such funds would cause responsible motorists to reduce the limits of liability insurance they carry; would abolish the accident-deterring effect of the safety responsibility law; would promote litigation and offer temptations to "fraud, collusion, and sharp practices."

Controversy on Merits of Forced Insurance

The extent to which financial losses of innocent victims of traffic accidents are compensated or remain uncompensated is a subject of controversy, with few exact statistics to support the contentions advanced on either side to the argument. Proponents of compulsory insurance say uncompensated losses aggregate huge sums; opponents say the seriousness of the problem is exaggerated for the purpose of generating support for mandatory insurance. . . .

The proportion of motorists covered by liability insurance varies widely from state to state. Available evidence indicates that where weak financial responsibility statutes are in effect approximately 30 per cent of the motorists will voluntarily insure themselves against damage claims. When the state adopts a strong safety responsibility law, carrying penalties that serve as an inducement to voluntary coverage, the ratio climbs within a few years to 60 per cent or more.

In New York and California, an estimated 90 to 95 per cent of the motorists are covered; in New Mexico, approximately 70 per cent; in Texas, approximately 60 per cent. But even under the strongest law, short of compulsory insurance for all drivers, there appears to be a residue of at least 5 per cent who fail to protect themselves against damage claims.

Much of the current debate on automobile liability laws revolves around the relative effectiveness of the two types of laws —compulsory insurance and safety responsibility—in reducing the number of accidents and in persuading motorists to purchase full insurance coverage. To the average car owner who buys insurance as routinely as he buys gasoline, the proposition that all motorists should be required to assume similar responsibility without waiting for a first accident makes a strong appeal, and sympathy for accident victims easily generates support for stringent legislation. Such support is held by opponents of compulsory insurance laws to be based on superficial considerations. . . .

Opponents of compulsory insurance legislation contend that it merely exacts payment of a fee for the privilege of driving recklessly, while a financial responsibility law "segregates those motorists who have been judicially found careless . . . and imposes restrictions on this class alone." A representative of the AAA told the Hults committee [of the New York legislature]:

The safety responsibility law is the only one of the [various] types of legislation that has or purports to have any deterrent effect upon reckless and financially irresponsible drivers. Compulsory insurance must, in the very nature of its concept, return the reckless and accident-prone driver to the stream of traffic, no matter how certain it may be that he will sooner or later be the cause of other accidents.

The deterrent effect of safety responsibility laws depends, it is admitted, on strict enforcement, and the goal of removing unsafe drivers from the road is obstructed by any laxity on the part of authorities.

The spirit [of the law] is thwarted by the widely recognized practice of pleading violations of the motor vehicle laws as crimes of a lesser type than originally charged at the time of arrest [one authoritative study of the subject made by the American University Law College has pointed out]. Enforcement officials and prosecuting attorneys are frequently content to dispose of their cases by agreeing to accept a plea of guilty to a minor traffic violation in preference to insisting that the trial proceed on a serious charge which, in the event of conviction, would lead to suspension of driving privileges and thereby invoke the safety responsibility law.

Major objections raised against compulsory insurance, aside from those based on considerations of safety, are that: (1) it is socialistic in concept; (2) it invites political interference; (3) it causes insurance premium rates to go up; (4) it fails to close major gaps in coverage under present legislation. . . .

Insurance companies fear that under compulsory systems unscrupulous politicians would be tempted to make campaign promises to lower insurance rates, and that eventually the profit margin of the underwriters would disappear and the state would be forced to take over. The compulsory system is said also to lend itself "to use by politicians whose friends might otherwise be ruled off the road." . . .

Insurance men frequently refer to the Massachusetts system as a "political football," and cite the following facts to support their contention. The state insurance commissioner resigned in 1928 because of a conflict between rate demands of the voters and the insurance companies, stating that the situation was "the result of an attempt to solve a mathematical problem by the introduction of a factor of political expediency." A special session of the Massachusetts legislature was called in 1931 to deal with rate revision. In 1935, to keep rates from climbing too high, coverage for guest occupants of cars was eliminated. A candidate for governor in 1936 made a campaign promise of rate reduction. A referendum was held in 1950 on the question of abolishing territorial differentials and establishing premium rates on a flat state-wide basis. Governor Herter in his 1953 message to the legislature said: "The operation of our compulsory automobile

insurance law has been a source of constant vexation to the
people."

Compulsory insurance in Massachusetts is further charged
with having caused an exaggerated tendency to file damage
claims, with resultant hikes in premium rates. The number of
damage suits involving use of automobiles more than doubled in
the first half year after the law went into effect and the population in some metropolitan areas is still regarded as uncommonly
"litigious." A New York *Times* study . . . showed that bodily
injury claims per 100 insured vehicles in Boston were twice as
high as in New York City, which itself has a relatively high rate
of claims filed. The Massachusetts law "has encouraged the most
honorable in the event of an accident to subscribe to the standard
that it is poetic license to collect money from an insurance company without any regard for integrity, liability, or the genuine-
ness of alleged injury and damage sustained." Premium rates in
Boston are among the highest in the nation, second only to New
York City.

To meet criticism of gaps in the protection afforded accident
victims under the usual state liability law, certain insurance companies have presented their own plan to assure blanket coverage.
It calls for establishment of a nonprofit Motor Vehicle Responsibility Insurance Corporation in which all companies writing
automobile insurance would participate. Motorists who already
carry automobile liability insurance and persons not owners of
cars could purchase insurance from the corporation to compensate
for their own personal injuries or property losses. Sponsors assert
that protection up to $5,000/$10,000/$1,000 (with a deduction
of $300 for first costs to be assumed by the insuree) could be
carried at a cost of 2 per cent of the basic premium for motorists
and of $2 a year for non-car owners.

The insurance group maintains that this plan is consistent
with established insurance principles, avoids state funding, eliminates the threat of state usurpation of the insurance business, and
offers wider coverage at a lower cost than compulsory liability insurance. But the Hults committee . . . turned down the proposal
on the ground that it failed to penalize the irresponsible driver;
would place an inequitable burden of at least $6 million on in-

sured motorists and $2 million on non-car owning families in the lower income brackets; it might force insured persons to hire counsel to obtain recovery from their own insurance companies. Furthermore, the committee doubted that any high percentage of insured motorists would buy the extra protection.

In general laws in the United States pertaining to motorists' financial responsibility are based on the common law principle that damages can be collected only from a person proved to be negligent or otherwise at fault. [A departure from this principle is found in the "comparative negligence" laws of five states (Georgia, Mississippi, Nebraska, South Dakota, Wisconsin) which allow claimants to collect, despite a showing they were negligent, if it is proved the other party showed greater negligence, as might be established by convictions for reckless driving, driving while drunk, or similar offenses.] There is growing support, however, for a contrary theory designed to meet the special problem of automobile accidents and already in force in the Canadian province of Saskatchewan.

Under the Saskatchewan plan a state compensation fund has been established from which damages, according to a specified indemnification schedule, are awarded to victims of accidents, without regard to negligence or fault. In adopting this method of compensation, the provincial legislature held that there was no effective solution to the problem of meeting the financial hazards of the road on an individual accident basis, that a certain number of accidents are bound to occur, and that all victims should be compensated as a matter of social welfare. The compensation fund is supported by charging vehicle owners an additional fee when their cars registered. . . .

A second plan originating in Canada that has been effective in inducing more motorists to purchase liability insurance is finding support in this country. Three Canadian provinces (Alberta, British Columbia, Manitoba) impound the cars of owners who fail to show financial responsibility in the event of an accident, regardless of cause or fault. The law is believed largely responsible for a great increase in voluntary insurance taken out by motorists in the three provinces. The New York Chamber of Commerce has recommended similar impounding authority, coupled with the insurance industry's proposal for self-coverage by motorists and pedestrians, as an effective means of diminishing losses due to uncompensated damages.

OUR LAGGARD LIABILITY LAWS [5]

We Americans are the world's greatest builders of automobiles and super-highways, but our system of handling lawsuits arising from automobile accidents is as old-fashioned as the original one-cylinder horseless carriage.

After more than twenty years on the bench, I am convinced that it is time—well past time, in fact—to get automobile-accident lawsuits out of our overburdened courts and to dispose of them in a sound and up-to-date manner patterned after the universally accepted system of workmen's compensation. This, as I will explain later, would mean that anyone injured in such an accident would be assured of compensation within a short time and on the basis of established payment schedules administered by a state board, without regard for the question of who was at fault in the accident. Such a system would eliminate the risk that injured persons, after years of litigation, may get no compensation at all, and it would, in my opinion, be fairer to all who become involved in an accident.

As a judge, I have no hesitation in saying that in our modern civilization almost anyone, including yourself, can end up in court in connection with a suit to recover damages suffered in an automobile accident, no matter how carefully you drive or even if you don't drive at all. And once you are in court you may well find yourself in for some real surprises.

Let me, for example, tell you about the case of the U-turn. At fourteen minutes past ten o'clock on a gray morning in January, Frederick K. Browne was driving on a wide road near Bergen, New Jersey, when he decided to turn around. He slowed down to fifteen miles an hour, observed that there was nobody

[5] From "Let's Put Sense in the Accident Laws" by Samuel H. Hofstadter, Justice of the New York Supreme Court, with Joe Alex Morris, magazine writer and former managing editor of *Collier's*. *Saturday Evening Post*. 228:17+. October 22, 1955. Reprinted by permission.

behind him, and then turned left to the center of the road. Coming from the opposite direction was a lumber-company truck driven by Peter V. Cross. Browne stopped in or near the center of the road and his car was struck by the truck driven by Cross. Mrs. Browne, riding in the front seat, was killed. A friend, Edgar F. Williams, who owned the automobile, was in the back seat and escaped with minor injuries. Browne himself was knocked unconscious and severely injured.

Two months later, three suits for damages were brought against the truck owner. One was by Browne, seeking $50,000 damages on the ground that the truck driver was negligent; another was by Browne as administrator of his wife's estate, seeking $60,000; and the third was by Williams, seeking $1500 for damage to his automobile. The truck owner was insured, and lawyers for the insurance company replied that it was Browne rather than the truck driver who had been negligent. No settlement being possible, the case was ordered tried before a jury. But the courts were overcrowded and it was more than three years before Browne and Williams had their pleas for damages presented in a courtroom over which I presided.

After hearing testimony from both sides, the jury decided that Browne could not recover any damages because he was guilty of contributory negligence. Legally, contributory negligence means that in some way the damaged party was at fault. In most states a plaintiff guilty of contributory negligence cannot collect damages under the strict interpretation of the law—not even if his negligence was only 1 per cent as compared to 99 per cent on the part of the defendant. The jury also decided that Williams, who, as owner of the car, had permitted Browne to drive, was indirectly guilty of contributory negligence and could not recover for damage to his automobile.

But then the jury decided that Browne, in his separate action as administrator of his wife's estate, was entitled to collect $25,000 as a result of the death of Mrs. Browne. This was possible under the law which "required" the jury to assess just compensation for the estate—in this case, for Browne and two children— if the truck driver was guilty of negligence in the accident which caused her death, and regardless of whether Browne had been negligent in any way. . . .

The point I want to make is that we, the people of New York, of Arizona, of Oregon, of Ohio and of every other state are attempting to employ a body of law that dates back to the Industrial Revolution in cases that call for an entirely new legal concept—a concept that should be as up-to-date as the 1956 automobile models. As a result of our old-fashioned approach, we have imposed absurdities and injustices on many persons involved in accidents. And—this is purely incidental—we have clogged our jury calendars with thousands of unnecessary cases, caused delays that run as high as four or five years in disposition of claims and wasted many thousands of dollars of taxpayers' money that might better have been used elsewhere.

I make such statements because I am convinced that the whole problem can be resolved by removing automobile-accident lawsuits from the courts and handling them in the same way that we handle factory accidents under workmen's compensation.

If this seems at first glance to be a radical solution, let us recall that the idea of workmen's compensation was a radical and bitterly opposed innovation only a generation or so ago, but that it has since been accepted as an essential part of our modern industrial civilization and that the objections originally raised against it have largely vanished into thin air. The principle of workmen's compensation is simply that industry must bear the cost of accidents which are bound to happen in factories. Today, in all forty-eight states, industries are required by law to carry liability insurance. If a workman is injured, he is awarded compensation by a state board in accordance with established schedules, but without any attempt to establish who was to blame for the accident. Thus lawsuits and the courts, are eliminated, the cost of compensation is equitably distributed, the injured workman is not subjected to the chance of getting nothing from a jury that might find him even 1 per cent negligent, and payment is made within a matter of weeks instead of years.

In applying the same principle to injuries suffered in an automobile accident, it would be necessary to require all motor-vehicle owners to carry liability insurance. Awards for injuries or damages would be made by a state compensation board on the basis of established schedules and without regard for the question of negligence, except in rare cases such as willful intent to injure. Awards would be paid by insurance companies or, if necessary, from state insurance funds such as have sometimes been set up for workmen's-compensation payments. The cost of administering the system—estimated at about 2 per cent of the total cost to policyholders—would be included in the automobile owners' premium payments to insurance companies. In the long run, the system might well save money both for the state and for the car owner. The state would save by eliminating a large percentage of personal-injury cases now in the courts. Premiums to car owners possibly would be less because of a decrease in the costly legal processes for which insurance companies must pay today. . . .

Automobile-accident compensation is intrinsically sound because of the drastic changes that have taken place in our way of life during the last half century. Even in 1923, when there were 15 million automobiles registered in the United States and when 14,411 persons were killed in automobile accidents, the problem was not acute all over the nation. But today we are a nation on wheels that turn with great speed on broad highways. Our annual toll of deaths in automobile accidents is close to 40,000. In 1954, for example, there were 1,307,000 automobile accidents in which 1,960,000 persons were injured and 35,500 killed. Our courts were buried under thousands of suits for personal damage due to such accidents. And, still forced to operate on the basically unsound theory that automobile accidents should be dealt with in the same fashion as the general run of accidents, our courts come up with some fantastic decisions. Only this year, for instance, a Circuit Court jury in Greenville, Mississippi, heard a case in which two drivers who had collided accused each other of blame. The jury awarded damages of $1000 to both parties on the ground that they were "equally negligent and suffered approximately equal injuries and damages."

In this connection, I should point out that our legal backwardness in handling such accident cases has been widely recognized and that trends have been established which are intended to help correct the inequity of our outdated system. Jurors often are unsympathetic toward the harsh rule of law that says a man who is negligent in even the slightest degree cannot collect damages. Many judges no longer hold this rule in the reverence it once commanded and in recent years an effort has been made to substitute a doctrine of "comparative negligence" for that of "contributory negligence." These are steps in the right direction, but they are only halfway measures that cannot solve the real problem. Nor can compulsory insurance laws alone, such as have been enacted in Massachusetts, be the answer, because the damaged individual must still prove that the accident was entirely the fault of the other party if he expects to be compensated.

And that is the heart of the whole matter. The concept that an automobile accident is due to individual fault is utterly unrealistic in modern civilization. It defies common sense and everyday experience. It fails to consider that, from an actuarial standpoint, such accidents are inevitable and that they should be considered on the same legal basis as accidents that occur in factories. Or let me put it another way: Society demands and needs the automobile and, in fact, could not do without it any more than it could do without our great industrial plants. Experience shows that no matter how carefully people drive or how stringent the traffic laws there will be automobile accidents. Therefore, society must accept collective responsibility for such accidents. They are a common burden of our society and should be dealt with on a collective rather than an individual basis, due to their unique character in our social and economic life. . . .

Under a state-administered system of compensation the injured party would simply apply to the compensation board, fill out the necessary forms and attend a hearing before an examiner, who would award payment for injuries on the basis of established schedules. There would, of course, be various schedules covering average income, time lost from work, partial disability, permanent disability, death, unemployed persons, minors, housewives and so on. The proceedings should require only a few weeks—instead of possibly years in the courts—and the injured person would be required to accept the board's award, except in certain unusual circumstances when it might be necessary to resort to regular court procedure.

Some years ago an exhaustive study of automobile-accident compensation was made by a special committee of the Columbia University Council for Research in the Social Sciences. It found the present system "inadequate to meet existing conditions" and showed by case studies that uninsured owners pay for only a very small proportion of the damage caused by their automobiles. "The committee," the report said, "favors the plan of compensation with limited liability and without regard to fault, analogous to that of the workmen's-compensation laws. It would be workable, its cost to motor-vehicle owners need not be unreasonable and it would not violate the due-process clause of the Constitution."

To which I can only add a hearty "Amen." Our legal processes should have caught up with the Automobile Age years ago. The law is not a strait jacket and the time has come for a fresh approach to this problem in harmony with our present-day needs.

FAST ROADS AND SLOW TRAFFIC [6]

We must modernize our traffic laws or prepare to accept less than full value for the . . . Federal highway program we are about to undertake. [For details on the new Federal program see Section III, below.—Ed.]

Although the cost of new regulations would be negligible, modernization in this field may be more difficult than raising billions for construction. It will mean upsetting some time-honored ideas in highway control.

Ever since the first automobile chugged its noisy way among the startled horses and amazed public, the motor car has been subjected to every restrictive traffic law conceived by man. There has been a concerted effort to curtail its movements with stop signs, traffic signals and speed limits. This attitude is already costing us much of the advantage we might gain from improved

[6] From "Slow Traffic Laws Waste Fast Roads" by J. Edward Johnston, Highway Transportation Specialist, Chamber of Commerce of the United States. *Nation's Business.* 44:32-3+. April 1956. Copyright 1956 by *Nation's Business.*

automobiles and highways. Unless we think more in terms of "go" than "slow" in drafting regulations, it is going to cost us more.

If we are to have effective traffic control we need to answer several basic questions:

Are current traffic regulations realistic?

Do they recognize the trend toward higher speeds and the need for uninterrupted flow of traffic?

Are speed limits high enough to insure that a violation is a gross misdemeanor or do they make violators out of reasonable drivers?

Is enforcement too rigid for less important traffic law infractions and not rigid enough for serious offenses?

Hundreds of studies show that the answer to these questions is no. Today the majority of our drivers are consistently violating the legal speed limits. This doesn't mean that the motorists are willful law breakers. It does mean that something is wrong with our regulations.

These traffic studies also bring out a number of basic principles which need to be observed if we are to get full benefit not only from the roads we are planning to build but from those we already have. Among them are these:

Most autoists drive reasonably and properly most of the time and are capable of recognizing conditions that require greater caution.

This view is not widely held. A recent poll of enforcement officials, motor vehicle administrators, members of traffic commissions and safety officials asked this question, among others: "Is it your impression that the driving public has generally demonstrated the ability to judge safe speeds of travel under all highway conditions?" Eighty per cent answered no.

These authorities see mainly the speeder and traffic violator and they investigate most traffic accidents. Granted that there are too many of each of these and they should be dealt with, they represent a small percentage of the normal driving public. Few drivers are serious traffic offenders and fewer still become involved in accidents.

Speed limits aimed at the few grossly reckless drivers make law violators out of normally good drivers and are of questionable value in controlling the violators.

Unrealistic traffic laws, if obeyed, increase delay and congestion but do little to solve the speed problem.

One city was having trouble with teen-agers racing hot rods through its streets. One suggested cure was to impose an unusually low city-wide speed limit—although the racing was done at speeds far exceeding the law already in effect.

Another city attacked the same problem by changing the stop signs from the cross streets to the arterial streets.

Of course, neither of these remedies worked. Such problems can be solved only on an individual basis through working with the parents of the youths involved, or through the schools, and by enforcing the speed laws already in effect.

But the public is permitting similar, unrealistic, traffic control almost daily throughout the nation.

Speed limits must be reasonable to be observed.

Low limits do not necessarily mean low speeds.

Studies have proven that drivers pay little or no attention to unreasonable speed limits. A small southern city had an unreasonable limit of 25 miles an hour. Surveys of one section of this road showed 90 out of every 100 drivers were exceeding the limit. On another section, 80 out of every 100 were doing so, in spite of the fact that the road was heavily patrolled and arrests were frequent.

In a speed study in a small midwestern city along a normally high speed highway, the limit was set at 35 miles an hour, then 40, 45, 50 and 55. Each limit was left in place several months to permit those who used the road regularly to get used to it. Furthermore, periods with no speed limit were used between changes in the maximum. There was little or no enforcement while the study was made.

The results showed that, whether the limit was 35 or 55 or unlimited, the difference in average driving speed was only four miles an hour. What is more when the limit was 35, some 18 per cent of the drivers went more than 50. When the limit was

50 only six per cent exceeded it.   Maximum voluntary observance
was found when the realistic speed limit was used.

*A reasonable speed limit is one that will include the speed of
all but a few of the fastest drivers.*

Many traffic authorities agree that a limit which includes 85
per cent of the drivers is reasonable. A speed limit should seem
too high to the majority of drivers.

If this is not the drivers' reaction, the limit is not maximum.
The limit should apply only to those who are grossly negligent,
taking into account allowances necessary for variables in speed-
ometers and arresting techniques—and this tolerance does not
need to be 10 to 15 miles an hour as is often the case.

Modern traffic does not adapt itself to fixed regulations. For
instance, a reasonable speed on any section of street and highway
may vary many times in the course of twenty-four hours. Speed
is affected by the amount and character of the traffic, weather and
lighting conditions. Furthermore, a reasonable speed often varies
from block to block or mile to mile because of changes in the
type and width of pavements, the presence of businesses, homes
and schools, grades, curves, etc. Yet, blanket speed limits have
been laid down covering wide areas, even entire states for all
hours of the day or night and all weather and traffic conditions.
Enforcement is then expected to uphold the law. . . .

Radar and other electric speed measuring devices can be
effective in speed enforcement if speed laws are realistic.

Most of our speed laws were not designed to be enforced by
devices that make accurate speed measurement possible. Wide
tolerances were expected between the posted limits and the speed
at which an arrest would actually be made. Such devices as radar
make possible the arrest of every driver exceeding a speed limit
by even one mile per hour. The wholesale arrest of drivers for
minor infractions that this makes possible was not the lawmakers'
intention.

Speed limits should encourage uniform speeds.

If all traffic moved at the same speed, there would be no over-
taking and passing—which results in a large number of fatalities
and injuries. The greatest tendency toward uniformity is achieved

when no more that 15 per cent of the drivers exceed the clearly posted speed limit.

There is no such thing as a safe speed limit.

Accidents and fatalities occur at all speeds. Actually records show that more traffic accidents and fatalities occur at speeds below 45 miles an hour than above; a large percentage of them happen at speeds below 35 miles an hour. . . .

B. W. Marsh, director, Traffic Engineering and Safety Department, American Automobile Association has said:

Rapid movement with reasonable safety is the goal in transportation. Since fatalities occur at almost all rates of movement, when does the rate become the "speed that kills," incompatible with sound transportation? Until this question has been satisfactorily answered, we should not be too dogmatic as to a specific speed limit.

Examples that are used to show drastic traffic accident reduction after a speed limit has been lowered, frequently fail to take all the facts into consideration. In a recent example a 60 m. p. h. limit was reduced to 50 on a section of road where traffic accidents had been unusually high. One year later traffic accidents were down 35 per cent.

But studies showed that the lower limit had not reduced vehicle speeds one bit. There had been an intensive enforcement program and safety educational campaign. Neither the lower speed limit nor the enforcement program had reduced speeds, but the program had made the driving public conscious of the need for caution on this stretch of highway. They did not drive more slowly but they did drive more cautiously. . . .

Many factors are more important than speed in causing accidents.

Traffic accidents have a definite cause and definite remedy. They are not really accidents at all.

Chance crack-ups—in the main those resulting from a tire or mechanical failure—are only a small percentage of the total. Most accidents result from an accumulation of circumstances which are more than the driver can cope with. For example, a driver approaching an uncontrolled intersection at the same time three other drivers approach it on the other streets has nine decisions to make within a matter of seconds. He must decide which of three possible movements each vehicle will take—straight through, left, or right. A driver who approaches at a reasonable speed has time to decide. But most speed limits would be too fast.

No traffic regulation can compensate for inattention, aggressiveness, pride of power, revenge, haste, condemnation, recklessness, daring and other traits. These are reflected in driving on the wrong side of the road, cutting in, failure to yield right of way, following too close, weaving from one lane to another, stopping too quickly and, yes, driving too fast for conditions.

Only traffic signal systems that are sensitive to variable traffic requirements should be used. Fixed time signal controllers, particularly those without programming devices, create untold delay. . . .

Stricter enforcement is needed for many traffic violations formerly considered minor.

On heavily traveled arterials, stopping, except for emergencies, should be a gross violation of the law.

Drivers should not be permitted to drive too slowly. They are often more of a menace than fast drivers.

Many drivers smugly feel that they are the only safe drivers in the traffic stream because they leave four car lengths between themselves and the car ahead even though two would be enough. If each car took up twice as much room . . . as it needed, think of the congestion.

The driver who holds back when approaching a red light is also using street space unnecessarily.

Changing from one lane to another if done with caution should not be condemned. Moving into a less congested lane makes better use of street space, fills up a less used lane and leaves a space in the lane just left for the traffic behind.

Restriction of left turns and also, where there are pedestrians, right turns, is vital in expediting traffic flow through critical areas.

In short we need to get rid of outmoded concepts of traffic and enforcement if the expanded road building program is to accomplish the purpose for which it is intended.

The future of automotive transportation can be bright if we match dollars for roads with realistic traffic regulations. The green light is due for a longer interval.

FORTY-EIGHT WAYS TO GET ONE TICKET [7]

Launching of the new . . . Federal highway program puts fresh urgency into an old question: What's going to be done to straighten out the jumble of conflicting state traffic laws?

The new highway-building program will open broad new avenues to the millions of interstate motorists. Will the traffic pattern they find on these highways in 1960 be tangled up in a 1916-model confusion of legal intricacies and contradictions?

Every motorist who has crossed a state line has run into exasperating—and dangerous—inconsistencies. In reconsidering its own traffic laws, a New York State legislative committee recently surveyed the comparable laws of all forty-eight states. It found that in Washington and Oregon the car entering an intersection from the right always has the right of way; down the coast, in California, it goes to whichever gets there first. Thirty-eight states require a driver to turn left *before* he reaches the center of an intersection. The other ten are equally firm in demanding that he turn *after* reaching the center, with Tennessee describing what is law in the other thirty-eight as "recklessness." Only twenty-five states have laws providing that cars must drive to the right of a rotary traffic circle. Most drivers, when they see a left arm fully extended, expect the car ahead to make a left turn, but in Pennsylvania and Michigan it can mean anything: start, stop, or a turn in either direction. Iowa drivers are taught not to park within five feet of a fire hydrant, or seven feet of a stop sign. But when they cross into Illinois they find that the limits are fifteen and thirty feet.

In most states parking is legal within eighteen inches of the curb. But in New York, New Jersey and Pennsylvania, the limit is six inches. A driver who backs up in Ohio breaks the law if he doesn't sound a warning first. Twenty-one states al-

[7] From "Those Crazy, Mixed-up Traffic Laws," editorial. *Collier's.* 138:94. September 14, 1956. Reprinted by permission.

low parking on bridges; twenty-seven forbid it. And though children in most states expect to have all traffic stop while a school bus is loading or unloading, the New York committee found that drivers from Colorado, Utah and the District of Columbia are not used to stopping.

The Chevy Chase Circle, on the outskirts of Washington, D.C., lies on the border between the District and Maryland. In the District of Columbia, the car *in* a traffic circle has the right of way. But according to Maryland law the car *entering* has the right of way. . . .

We have the means to straighten out the present legislative jumble. All we lack, seemingly, is the will.

Thirty years ago—in 1926—a committee under the Secretary of Commerce [Herbert Hoover] distilled the best of each state's laws into a single Uniform Vehicle Code. That code has since been constantly reviewed and revised to keep it abreast of the changing patterns of traffic. Its adoption by the states has been urged by, among others, the American Automobile Association, the Bureau of Public Roads, the United States Chamber of Commerce, the National Safety Council and the National Highway Users Conference. The latest Governors' Conference named a special committee under Connecticut's Governor Abraham Ribicoff to begin a new study aimed at adoption of uniform laws and uniform enforcement among the states.

The thirty years of campaigning for adoption of the Uniform Vehicle Code covers more than half the automotive history of the United States. But thirteen state legislatures have still refused, or haven't bothered, to bring their rules of the road even into "substantial" agreement with those set forth in the code. The result has been a legislative hodgepodge that makes it virtually impossible for the conscientious interstate driver to know what laws apply in the place where he is. Add the radical differences in the degree of enforcement among various states and communities, and we have a fabric of regulation and nonregulation that can't help but undermine basic respect for the law itself.

One of the fundamental reasons for having traffic laws at all is to establish a degree of uniformity, and therefore of predictability, in the driving habits of those motorists with whom we're going to share the road. But where is our predictability when a left-hand-turn signal in New York may mean a right-hand turn in Pennsylvania? Or when a driver with the right of way under Oregon law comes to an intersection and meets another driver who has the right of way under his native California law? And what, we may wonder, will happen to the flow of traffic if ever a law-abiding Marylander about to enter the Chevy Chase Circle meets an equally conscientious Washington driver already in it—so that each is required to wait for the other?

In the days when a twenty-five-mile trip was a major undertaking, we could afford to indulge local whims in the making of traffic laws. But today hardly anyone does all his driving within a single state. Automobile designers have superbly anticipated the motoring needs of a nation that has telescoped yesterday's journey into a jaunt today. Those who plan our highways have at least followed closely behind these needs. But the makers of our laws have seemed to ignore one basic principle of traffic regulation: it matters less what the rules of the road are than it does that everyone driving on the same roads drive by the same rules.

Don McClaugherty, chairman of the Uniform Laws and Safety Committee of the Highway Transportation Congress, has estimated that eliminating the present jumble of conflicting state traffic laws could reduce road accidents by 30 per cent. Even allowing for Mr. McClaugherty's possible optimism, there can be no doubt that at least a significant part of the 38,000 persons who died last year in automobile accidents would still be alive if we had had one set of rules that all drivers could follow.

OUR STRANGLING HIGHWAYS [8]

To some people the United States is not seen as people, but as a gigantic skeleton of hard-surface roads crawling with motor vehicles. Seen in this way the mammoth web of concrete is a

[8] From an article by David Cort, a frequent contributor to *Nation* and other magazines. *Nation*. 182:357-60. April 28, 1956. Reprinted by permission.

monstrosity. But the monstrosity is necessary, say the big thinkers, because 70 million American car-owners are daily impelled to drive an average of twenty-five miles—a statistical total of 1.7 billion per day. Even if half or three quarters of this traffic were utterly unnecessary and unprofitable to everybody, they say, it must be maintained and encouraged. The reason? American prosperity depends on perpetual boom in the automobile industry and the production and sale of 8 million new cars every year.

It may be time these articles of faith were more closely examined. The crisis of a fatal illness attacking the country is adequately, though unintentionally, described in a new publicity book issued by Henry Ford II, *Freedom of the American Road*, plus the current news about toll roads. Mr. Ford's foreword justifies the fine title in a sentence that will be returned to later: "We Americans have always liked . . . freedom to come and go as we please in this big country of ours." However, the freedom he is discussing is only the "freedom" under license to drive a motor vehicle on a roadbed never paid for by the automobile industry. A licensed right is never an absolute, sovereign right. The use of the word "freedom" in this context is a play on words, perhaps a dangerous joke. [For extracts from *Freedom of the American Road* see "The Past Is Prologue," in Section I; "If War Should Come," in this section, below; and "The Battle for Highways—In California," in Section III.—Ed.]

The book makes clear that America's present road-building boom began hardly ten (nearer five) years ago. In that interval little bands of patriots arose in such localities as California, New Jersey, Pennsylvania, North Carolina, Oregon, Washington, Maine, Boston, Portland (Oregon), San Francisco, Detroit, Albuquerque, Pittsburgh, Los Angeles, Dallas and Atlanta. Their communities were being strangled to death by traffic. Like modern Herculeses, they saved their world by epic labors and legislations. Henry Ford's writers raise them to the highest echelon of peacetime American heroes. One can hardly criticize anything they did; besides, now it is done. . . .

Some of the expressways are over four hundred feet wide. The New York Thruway is generally two hundred feet wide; rural hard-surface roads run between thirty and fifty feet wide from margin to margin, including shoulders, ditches and verges. If the average works out at only fifty feet, the total acreage taken over by United States roads is forty thousand square miles—a good deal more than the area of the five New England states, excluding Maine.

I do not resent this loss. For the sake of communication among all the forty-eight states, we can afford to liquidate five or six. The fact is given only to put a going value on this communication and pose the question of how much more calcified skeleton, how much more monstrosity, we can reasonably afford.

The Ford book for all its enthusiasm gives the unexpected effect of tracing a dreadful disease over the body of America. Pullulating bumper to bumper, unassimilable organisms were about to kill the victim; then the doctors stepped in and accelerated the flow. No wonder the treatments invariably conclude on an ominous diagnosis. . . .

This ominous note is fully justified. It is doubtful whether a continuously multiplying traffic load could be handled by doubling our forty thousand square miles of roads. Eighty thousand square miles? Two hundred thousand? Five hundred thousand? The United States has only three million square miles, many of them unsuitable for highways. But the crux is in the cities. Adequate roads there obviously demand the flattening of at least half the buildings in our metropolises. End of joke.

The problem is not people. True, the cities are full of people, but a walking human being needs only three square feet of surface at any one moment and the safety margin is important only for women with raised umbrellas. A slow-moving automobile needs a space eight by fifty feet for safety, or four hundred square feet. Hence, a city has a limit to the number of automobiles it can take. If all America's 75 million motor vehicles were on the road at the same time, they would require over 5 million miles of one-lane highway. The present roads could handle them if they would spread out evenly, moving slowly, over every existing road. But of course they don't, won't and can't. Most of them are always going to the same places—fast. Too many want to get into the same four hundred square feet. Since each driver has been encouraged to believe that he is entitled to this "Freedom of the American Road," the organisms pile up monstrously at critical points. The classic California pile-up was at Bayshore's Boneyard Hill— seventy-four vehicles in one gigantic crash. . . .

"Freedom of the road" recalls "the right of departure" lost by the Russian people after the Mongol conquest. This right has never been questioned for Americans. But should an American pedestrian claim "the right of departure" from New York City and try to go cross-country afoot, he would find himself confronted by the highways as by a net of Chinese walls. Notably in the Bronx and Queens, he is stopped by a great embankment. If he can, he clambers up it, only to face the peril of his life in a stream of cars plunging past him. At a break in that one-way traffic, he darts to the median line and teeters there watching the other-way traffic. This next dash may cost him his life.

Most municipal magistrates would be astonished to be informed that that pedestrian has an absolute right to cross that expressway. Municipal "jay-walking" ordinances are all essentially unconstitutional. The driver contests the pedestrian's right with only a *licensed* right. If the sovereign citizen, the proprietor of the road, scuttles across it, he scuttles only as a practical matter of survival, not in fear of violating any ordinance forbidding him to leave his viscera "spread out like strawberry jam." The driver's right depends on his observance of his responsibilities and the rights of other drivers and pedestrians. Like a licensed pistol-wearer, he is given the power of life or death over his fellow-citizen. Any sensible society naturally hedges such a right.

America's great problem is not even traffic but, as with every civilization that ever existed, to keep and curry the love of its citizens for the whole society and its arrangements. In an ancient Babylon, Egypt and Rome some of that love drained out of a citizen confronted with mammoth public works comparable to the Queens highway that stops the cross-country pedestrian. It is not very metaphysical to say that when a civilization intimidates, excludes and terrifies even one citizen, it is a little nearer its death.

These great highway structures cannot be loved, and are not. The East River Drive in Manhattan, for example, almost completely excludes pedestrian Manhattanites from the East River. Every expressway excludes a number of people from what they love on the other side of the road. Structural gigantism is a fairly sure way to kill the individual's love for his world.

This estrangement of the American family by gigantism may be the clue to the whole automobile problem. It may often be just this estrangement that gives the family head the compulsion to buy a car. His car identifies him with the gigantism. It is his car, with a bum carburetor, a few individual dents and some interior litter. When he rides out into the maelstrom, he reestablishes his part in the huge thing rushing past his door. This compels the civilization to build yet more gigantic highways and the citizen feels worse again.

The family drives out to visit Aunt Esther in Hempstead, whom they don't like, instead of dropping around the corner to see Aunt Myrtle, whom they do like; or to a restaurant twenty miles away that is worse than the one down two blocks. The real purpose of the trips is to get into the maelstrom, which they all pretend to hate.

The price they pay for their cars is ruinous. According to a crack car salesman, he will give a $4,000 car to a provably solvent customer for $3,600 nowadays. However, the price including insurance and carrying charges really comes to $4,200, if it is paid over three years. The car is worth about $2,500 practically as soon as it is driven out of the salesroom. At the end of one year, the customer will have paid $1,400, owe $2,800 and have a $2,000 car to show for it. A year's use costs him $2,200, excluding operating expenses.

We are told that Detroit must be kept happy, unless the United States is to go on the rocks. We have done our best with the subsidy of $10 billion a year for the roadbed for Detroit's products. It is not enough.

But if we can allow Detroit to take care of itself, there is a solution to the highway and traffic problem: fewer cars on the roads. The details:

1. Because a single bus or train takes between twenty and one thousand cars off the roads, we must certainly allocate subsidies to buses and, in particular, railroads. (The old anti-railroad prejudice, inherited from the land-grant period, is obsolete; Eastern railroads never got land grants.) Inter-city passenger traffic in 1953 was 86 per cent by car, 5.6 per cent by railroad and 5 per cent by bus. The railroads that year carried an average of about 1.5 million passengers every day, pulling off the roads about 1 million cars. If the railroads were equipped to carry around 20 million passsengers a day, the huge subsidies for highways could be cut down to size. The saving in gasoline, rubber and metal as well as nervous system would make America a rich and happy land.

The present auto mania is so appalling or ridiculous, depending on where your sense of humor lies, that even *urban* traffic is over 87 per cent by car and only 11 per cent by transit systems. Railroads won't solve this.

2. The privilege of driving a car must be made immensely more honorable and exclusive. License examinations must be rigorous.

3. Licenses must be suspended at the first violation of responsibility or first indication of incompetence. The suspension period ought to be in terms of years, not weeks.

4. Detroit must be required by law to build lower speeds into cars and trucks.

5. Ruinous terms of installment purchase must be outlawed.

6. Creation of central shopping districts cleared of motor vehicles and streets, except for underground service tunnels (as in the new Fort Worth plan). In Manhattan, for example, only people and subways would be admitted to an area at least from 34th to 59th Streets between Sixth and Lexington Avenues.

To these proposals I gladly add those submitted in the Henry Ford book by Robert Moses: movement of certain goods at night; staggered work hours; more parking meters; "adequate loading and unloading and off-street parking in all new buildings"; "public subsurface, surface and upper-level parking at reasonable rates"; "strategically located bus garages and truck terminals"; arcaded sidewalks to expand streets; "much more drastic zoning restrictions."

The Moses list might serve as interim measures while the railroads, bus lines, licensing bureaus and police departments are getting into position for the all-out solution.

Whether or not the answer has been given here, some solution is inevitable—and fairly soon. America is not a sick body; the disease of the automobile is only a metaphor. Otherwise, with such a disease, the patient would surely die. But it can be predicted that any solution must stop the propagation of more and more cars and roads.

The automobile may have converted the descendants of American pioneers, the toughest, most energetic and open-minded people in the civilized world, into lazy and fat-seated invalids in forty years. But it is yet to be proved that it has also made them fat-headed.

COLLECTING TOLLS WITH BOTH HANDS [9]

Recently a young Navy seaman at Portsmouth, Virginia, given a short leave, decided to visit his family in Massachusetts. Happily he climbed into his car and began the journey.

His automobile motor was barely warm when he was stopped and told to dig into his pocket for 30 cents for the Portsmouth-Norfolk tunnel. At Norfolk, he was stopped again and paid $1.25 for a five-minute ferry ride across Hampton Roads to Newport News. A few miles later, he paid 75 cents at a York River bridge. Soon there was a similar toll for him to pay at the Potomac River Bridge.

[9] From "Tired of Paying Highway Tolls?" by John L. Springer, feature and magazine writer. Reprinted by permission from *Coronet*. 34:42-6. June 1953. Copyright by Esquire, Inc. 1953.

Dazed by the parade of outstretched palms, the sailor drove on. He paid tolls on the Delaware Memorial Bridge, on the New Jersey Turnpike, on the George Washington Bridge spanning the Hudson, on the Henry Hudson Parkway, on roads up to Massachusetts. When he finally reached his home with a flattened purse, he added his expenditures.

On the 597-mile drive, he had paid $6.60 for tolls—over a cent a mile simply for the privilege of riding on roads and bridges. This was only $1.75 less than he had paid for gasoline and oil on the entire trip!

This shocking example of how toll collectors are taking over our travel facilities is not unusual. . . . Nine states, mainly in the East and Midwest, already are grabbing coins from motorists. Seventeen others have approved or proposed pay-as-you-ride highways. Soon, a motorist traveling from Maine to Minnesota will find a toll-taker's outstretched palm on almost every modern road he uses.

"What's wrong with that?" ask some supporters of toll roads. "Why shouldn't motorists pay for the roads they use?"

The answer, often overlooked by the public and by the victimized motorists themselves, is that motorists have *already paid in advance for toll roads through gasoline taxes*. And the appalling fact is that motorists who ride on toll roads usually pay for them not just twice, but *three* and *four* times!

When automobiles grew in popularity, state officials realized that better roads would be needed. "We'll tax the gasoline these cars use, and build roads with the money," they decided.

For years, this idea worked. Gasoline tax rates soared. As millions poured in, state politicians came up with another clever thought: "Let's use these taxes for things other than highways."

Thus began the sinister practice of diversion—the use of gas-tax money for purposes never originally intended. Since 1924, says the Federal Bureau of Public Roads, states have used $3 billion of motorists' taxes to grow oysters, support public cemeteries, operate ski schools, and for other purposes as far from road building as the mind can imagine.

In 1951, out of every dollar that poured into state treasuries in highway-use taxes, only 53 cents was used *directly* on highway work. Another 37 cents went for administration and tax collection costs, to state highway police and payments to holders of highway bonds. Yet in that year, states diverted $266,771,000 to other purposes. This sum could have built a modern, two-lane highway from New York to California—a *free road*.

Every year, the motorist pays for such a three-thousand-mile coast-to-coast highway—a road he never gets! "Since 1934," says the National Highway Users Conference, "121,487 miles of road could have been built with monies diverted by state governments"—the *equivalent to forty coast-to-coast highways!*

Through the years, needed roads remained unbuilt. Then, when highway congestion became so frightful that road building could no longer be delayed, state officials threw up their hands helplessly. "We don't have the money to build free roads," they said. "So we'll charge tolls for them."

But building a toll road is not like building a free road. Often, it is three or four times costlier.

First, consider the financing. Instead of paying for the roads out of their own treasuries, the states borrow the money. To attract investors, they pay high interest rates. . . . Secondly, toll roads are more expensive to build. Free roads open to the public may have many intersections. Toll roads must eliminate these to prevent motorists from coming onto the roads free. Costly overpasses must be built.

Third, hundreds of employees must be hired to man toll booths day and night.

Because of these factors, the American Automobile Association states flatly: "The per-mile cost of the toll road is substantially higher than the cost of an equivalent free road." Who pays? The poor, helpless motorist, of course.

Now consider another way in which toll roads milk the taxpayer. Bondholders who finance the roads usually demand that, to protect their investments, the profits from gasoline, restaurant and other sales be added to tolls collected. When new throughways open, they inevitably draw traffic from nearby highways. Often, private owners of gas stations, restaurants and roadstands along older roads are squeezed to death.

U S Highway 130 once was a bustling road, teeming with traffic from Philadelphia and the South to New York. A main link in the eastern coast highway system, it was used by big trailer-trucks and private cars. Along the highway, business prospered. Merchants spent millions to improve service stations, diners, motels. They paid out hundreds of thousands more in taxes.

Then the Jersey Turnpike opened. Business on U S 130 dropped at once. Motels which once served one hundred customers a night now served ten. Receipts of gas stations were halved. Dozens of taxpayers, who had spent years developing their businesses, were forced to sell out at huge losses.

The AAA warns that officials may "deliberately retard the improvement of free roads which compete with a toll highway, especially if a toll road is having trouble making ends meet." . . .

Despite the gross unfairness of most toll roads, many persons continue to praise them lavishly. Let us see why.

"These roads are marvels of scientific engineering," they argue. "They are generally far better than free highways. They are attractively landscaped, unmarred by billboards or other eyesores. They enable you to travel long distances speedily without traffic jams. Their advantages far outweigh the annoyance of having to pay tolls."

True, toll roads usually are better than existing free roads. If they weren't, motorists would not pay to use them. True, they are often more attractive. But only because state officials have misused the gas taxes that could have made free turnpikes attractive, too.

Also, on toll roads, speeds far greater than average are permitted. But is this an advantage? In a dozen years on the Pennsylvania Turnpike, 395 persons have died in accidents. In 1950 alone, there were 949 accidents, involving 1,641 vehicles. . . .

The idea of forcing motorists to pay to use government-built roads is recent. During the depression, public works projects were sought to make jobs. Why not blast a super-road through Pennsylvania's mountains and charge the public to ride on it? . . . In 1939—a year before the Pennsylvania road was even opened—Connecticut set up toll booths along its new Merritt Parkway. The snatch for dimes was on.

Today, toll roads already in operation, under construction, approved or proposed, total six thousand miles and involve twenty-six states: Colorado, Connecticut, Florida, Georgia, Illinois, Indiana, Iowa, Kansas, Kentucky, Maine, Maryland, Massachusetts, Missouri, New Hampshire, New Jersey, New York, North Carolina, Ohio, Oklahoma, Pennsylvania, Tennessee, Texas, Virginia, Washington, West Virginia and Wisconsin.

In nine states, individuals or agencies already have authority to build toll roads *at will*. In some, a highway department legally can designate toll routes as it pleases. In others, only the governor's approval is needed.

If officials propose a toll road in your state, ask what has happened to the gas tax revenues. Why can't these taxes pay for the road? If gas taxes have been diverted . . . states should not plead poverty and turn to tolls for an easy solution.

If a toll road appears needed, put traffic experts on record that the estimated volume will pay for it. Obviously, a toll road that cannot pay for itself should never be built. But such roads have already been put over on the public.

Make certain that once the toll road is paid for, it will be made available to the public *free*. Any bill your legislature passes authorizing a toll road should contain specific guarantees that the road will become a freeway when paid for.

TAX ROAD OR TOLL ROAD? [10]

The arguments against the toll road sound plausible. The driver who uses the toll road pays about one cent a mile for the privilege. If, instead of paying tolls, he paid 15 cents a gallon extra for his gasoline, his costs would be about the same. Why not have the state charge him that extra 15 cents a gallon in taxes and use the money to build free superhighways?

[10] From an article by George Koether, automotive editor of *Look*. Reprinted by permission from the June 16, 1953 issue of *Look* magazine, p76+. Copyright by Cowles Magazines, Inc. 1953.

Proponents of toll roads don't go along with this arithmetic, or with the conclusions based upon it. It is quite true, they admit, that the alternatives are the toll road or the tax road, for every road must be paid for. But the big difference, they contend, is that tax roads are financed by involuntary contributions and often built where politicians want them to go.

Toll roads, in contrast, are built where and when patronage makes them possible. The driver himself decides whether he is willing to pay the price. When he travels a toll road, he is making the same free choice he makes when he buys a ticket for a movie, a ball game or a train ride. The price system, in other words, is the application of free-enterprise principles to highway construction.

In a limited way, it is a return to first principles, for the first great era of road building in this country took place under a toll-road system.

Why did the toll road return? Economic necessity brought it back. "The toll-road movement," says economist Wilfred Owen of the Brookings Institution, "has developed out of the failure of public-highway management, because of political interference, to apply the tools available to it in a manner productive of effective highway development." This is a polite way of saying: "Public enterprise has failed, so state governments have returned to the principles of private enterprise— the price system."

This was the seed of treason to those who believe in the age-old theory that roads belong to the public and should thus be managed by the state. So toll roads have to fight their way over well-organized opposition. One high hurdle they had to surmount was the old-fashioned theory that high-speed highways, by-passing business districts, hurt trade. In 1950, the Massachusetts Turnpike Commision, in rejecting a toll-road proposal, flatly stated:

> The toll-road idea is not considered good policy because the road would be restricted to the few who could afford to pay. . . . Millions of dollars are spent here each year by out-of-state visitors. . . . It is not the desire of the members of this Commission . . . and also the businessmen, to quickly transport these visitors through the state. . . . Each out-of-

state visitor to Massachusetts has potential spending power and should be encouraged to remain. . . . A toll highway is not the economic solution of anything.

The public, however, felt otherwise. For in a survey of 34,510 motorists, 84.5 per cent said they would use a toll road if it were built. . . .

A similar reluctance to use the pay-as-you-ride principle was shown in the building of New York's Thruway. Originally the Thruway was planned as a "free" road. Ground was broken in July 1946. Three and a half years later, it became obvious that the Thruway's completion would be delayed for years if highway taxes were to be the only source of funds. Then New York turned to the toll principle, created a Thruway Authority and prepared to charge tolls.

The financial success of toll roads like the New Jersey Turnpike has helped to change the minds of highway officials. "I used to argue against toll roads," said a nationally known highway engineer, "but one night, after a speech, someone asked me: 'Have you ever, in all the years the Merritt Parkway has been operating, heard anyone object to paying the toll?' I hadn't—and I haven't. Since then, I refuse to argue against toll roads."

In fact, in their new-found love for the toll road, some legislators have begun a move to take over toll roads by a flank attack on the taxpayers' pocketbooks. Recently, a trend to what economists call "uneconomic" toll-road building has set in. That is, laws have been passed to permit states to build toll roads backed by *both* the revenue from tolls and the taxing power of the state. New Jersey's Garden State Parkway, for example, was sold to the voters on the theory that it would never cost them anything except tolls. Possibly, it may not. But in the event that tolls do not meet costs or interest payments on the bonds, New Jersey taxpayers will have to pay the charges through tax levies.

Is the toll road a magic answer to all of America's highway muddle? Only a few economists have had the courage to say yes. But some students of the problem, whose competence is above question, are pointing to the toll idea as a possible answer to the worst part of our traffic problem—urban congestion. If the toll idea works for intercity traffic, they are asking, why will it not work for heavy traffic in urban areas?

Harmer Davis, director of the Institute of Transportation and Traffic Engineering at the University of California, says: "An extensive system of urban arterials subject to toll-gate control would be a feasible operation." Davis would overcome the high cost of building toll-gate facilities in urban areas by installing some form of special licensing system like that in use on Connecticut's Merritt Parkway. Under this system, motorists wanting to use urban expressways would "subscribe" to the service by purchasing an annual plate which they could display on their cars, thus entitling them to entry on an expressway without bothering to pay the toll each time they used it. Brookings economist Wilfred Owen suggests the possibility of combining urban toll expressways with large offstreet parking centers.

A forum of experts in city planning recently concluded that the "price mechanism offers perhaps the one best hope of rationalizing the use of our downtown streets, just as the price mechanism has proved the one best means to balance supply and demand in every other line." Which is another way of saying that the pay-as-you-ride toll system is the answer.

One way or another, new urban and interstate highways will have to be built. And one way or another, the money must come from the pockets of average Americans. The question is: How shall it be collected? As the highways choke up, the nation's economy will be strangled. Toll road or tax road, we must get to work a-building.

BUMPY GOING FOR THE TOLL ROADS [11]

Inflation and politics have caused important shifts by the managers of some of the nation's toll roads.

First came the unsettling news that passenger car rates on the Pennsylvania Turnpike—oldest and most successful of the

[11] From "Bumpy Going for the Turnpikes." *Business Week.* p166+. June 9, 1956; and "Toll Roads: Is It the End of the Boom?" *Business Week.* p43-4. February 11, 1956. Reprinted by special permission of *Business Week,* a McGraw-Hill publication. Copyright 1956 by McGraw-Hill Publishing Company.

modern toll roads—would be upped 41 per cent over its whole length from the Ohio line to New Jersey. At the same time, truck rates would be cut about 20 per cent in an effort to draw the commercial traffic that is the meat and potatoes of any toll diet. . . .

The turnpike commissioners figure the moves will boost annual revenues by $4 million; the fact that a political hassle has held up the toll changes hasn't lightened the impact on other toll roads of the proposed passenger car boost, first of any consequence since the pike opened.

The need for more revenues did not arise from the main stretch of the road, the 327 miles from King of Prussia to Ohio. This stretch, knifing through some of the roughest mountain country in the East, has always more than paid its way. Since it was started in 1939-1940, it has built up an $18 million surplus, and is far ahead of the amortization schedule of the original $211.5 million bond issue.

But other, newer stretches—to Allentown in the north and across the Delaware River Bridge to the east—are not doing so well. And none of the surplus can be applied to them until the bonds on the original stretch are all paid off, probably not for another five or six years.

The commission itself listed these reasons for proposing the rate changes:

Weight limits on free roads have been adjusted, opening them to trucks that formerly had to use the turnpike. This has caused some attrition of pike traffic, especially in the less rugged areas in the eastern part of the state, and just west of Pittsburgh.

Route 22 has been widened and rebuilt east of Harrisburg, so that trucks prefer to leave the turnpike there and take the free road directly to New York, instead of staying on the pike to Philadelphia and then paying further tolls on the New Jersey Turnpike to reach the New York area.

Maintenance costs are rising all along the pike.

Truck traffic on the new extension from Valley Forge to the Delaware River Bridge has fallen far below engineers' estimates.

On all the new extensions, revenues are running about 40 per cent behind expectations, and bondholders are restive. Last year the extensions didn't earn even enough to pay interest on the $298 million issues that were floated to build them; 1956 prospects are even gloomier. The interest deficits are made up by a reserve fund, but under terms of the indenture, the bondholders' trustee—Fidelity-Philadelphia Trust Co.—can force the commission to boost tolls if deficits continue. There is no chance that revenues will meet this year's interest. If tolls aren't raised . . . the bank can order a sixty-day study of the situation, then force new tolls. It could even ask for lower tolls if the engineers recommended them. But odds now are that higher tolls will be the prescription.

As if the economics of the pike weren't confusing enough, state politics have muddled the picture further. The Turnpike Commission normally has five members, but there were two vacancies when the first vote was taken, O.K.'ing the higher tolls. Democratic Governor George M. Leader—with the backing of highly vocal auto clubs and Pennsylvania newspapers—assailed the moves. The two Democrats on the commission were willing to reverse the recommendatiton, but Republican member James F. Torrance, Jr., refused to back down. The governor then appointed another Democrat to the commission, which voted, 3 to 1, to put the higher rates in the icebox until further studies could be made.

Until the studies are made, by engineers and by the state senate, there will probably be no action on rates. However, considering the unsatisfactory performance of the eastern extensions something must be done—be it voluntary, or forced by the bondholders' trustee.

While Pennsylvania's legislators and politicians haggled over tolls, Connecticut's state expressway bond committee came out with an expected request for a boost in bond authorizations from $398 million to $447 million. The reason given was rising

cost of materials, construction, and land for the 129-mile Green-
wich-Killingly Expressway that's now being built. The road's
traffic engineers also estimated that tolls would have to be raised
before the road is even in operation. The proposed 20 cent
minimum for passenger cars would be raised to 25 cents.

Connecticut's struggle with costs is highlighted by Pennsylvania's experience on its unprofitable eastern extensions. For
instance, the stretch from Valley Forge to New Jersey cost
around $98 million—around $3 million per mile. This was in
1954. By contrast, the original 161-mile section of the pike cost
only $70 million, with nearly $30 million coming from Public
Works Administration funds, back in 1939. Cost per mile:
about $430,000.

Actually, costs of highway construction have risen as fast
in the past twelve months as in any similar postwar period;
Engineering News-Record's index of heavy construction stands
5.8 per cent higher this week than it did a year ago. Fast-rising
costs of construction and maintenance coupled with reports of
mediocre revenues on many roads, could put a crimp in plans
for future roads. . . .

End of the Boom?

Despite the probable slowdown in building, more toll road
bonds should come into the market in 1956 than in any previous year. That's because $3.6 billion of bonds scheduled for
1955 were postponed. Of these some $2.5 billion are expected
this year.

There were a number of reasons why all but $750 million
of 1955's scheduled bonds were held up. Politics tangled Connecticut's plans for a $100 million offering to extend its Green-
wich-Killingly Thruway. Legal action snarled a gigantic ($415
million) issue in Illinois after it had been sold but before delivery of the bonds to the investors. Other issues were affected
by changing cost estimates and by a tightening of the bond market. In all, thirteen states delayed plans for bond issues.

Some states that had held preliminary discussion of the
feasibility of toll roads decided to hold off any firm planning

until Congress acted. An even bigger factor for delay—perhaps the biggest of all—was the disconcerting failure of a few toll roads to live up to expectations.

Outstanding in the 1955 toll road story was the West Virginia Turnpike; . . . this sorry chapter drew more publicity that the roads that fared far better. The turnpike, financed by $133 million bonds, opened in November 1954 with much fanfare as a link between the Midwest and the fast-growing Southeast. The road winds through a mountainous area with practically no competing roads.

Coverdale & Colpitts, an engineering firm that has done the lion's share of toll road surveys, estimated that the West Virginia Turnpike's 1955 tolls would be $5,237,000, about 71 per cent of it to be provided by trucks. As the year wore on it became evident that the estimates were way high. By December, revenues had fallen short by $2.5 million and trucks were contributing only 31 per cent of the total. The bonds were selling nearly 30 points below their offering price.

Some engineers blame the showing on the poor condition of the roads at either end of the turnpike. Truckers, they say, see little sense in struggling over these bad roads just to use the eighty-eight miles of new road. . . .

One Wall Street banking house is already drafting plans for refinancing the pike, should the state decide such action might help.

Right now, the Judiciary Committee of the West Virginia House of Delegates is pressing an investigation of the pike. It has already urged the legislature to pledge the state's credit behind a new bond issue of some $200 million to extend the road to the north, and thus possibly bail it out.

Ohio is another state with toll road troubles, though not so acute as West Virginia's. The Ohio road has found truck revenues running substantially below estimates. Trucks have been expected to contribute 44 per cent of traffic and 73 per cent of tolls. Instead, in the first three months, trucks made up only 14 per cent of traffic and 32 per cent of tolls. Turnpike officials are weighing a cut in the truck tolls, which the carriers say are too high.

Ohio has throttled back on its long-planned North-South Turnpike, originally scheduled to cost around $525 million.

Engineers are now trying to eliminate between $170 million and $200 million of this projected construction, in order to make the road more palatable to investors.

Of late, investment bankers and long-term investors—notably life insurance companies—have been fixing a chillier eye on the toll road bonds, which they used to favor because of good yields bolstered by Federal tax exemption and steady earnings records. One underwriter explains the new caution this way: "We've passed the day when the mere mention of toll road bonds could cast an aura of enchantment—the whole situation is being very carefully appraised right now."

As knowledge of toll roads has increased, one bit of fiction has been laid to rest: the idea that the profitable toll road is a straight long line between two urban centers. Now one engineer says, "We have learned that there just ain't such a thing as long-haul traffic."

On the highly successful New Jersey Turnpike, lying between the nation's largest and third largest cities, the average trip is only one-third of the pike's length: only 6 per cent of traffic goes the whole way. On the Pennsylvania Turnpike, as new sections have been opened boosting the maximum possible toll, the actual average toll paid has risen at a much slower pace. When the pike reached its full length, the maximum toll had grown to $3.75, from the original $2. But the average toll climbed only 10 cents to a modest 95 cents.

The engineers have concluded that the most profitable toll road is a fairly short one between large commercial centers. But only a limited number of such routes remain to be built, which indicates another brake on future building.

According to some engineers the whole pattern of truck traffic is changing, and no large-scale toll projects should be undertaken until the trend becomes clear. For one thing, more and more drivers are being paid per trip, instead of per hour, which means that time as a factor is less important in figuring whether or not to use the faster, but more expensive, turnpike.

In some areas, the very excellence of the turnpikes has back-fired. The toll roads have attracted so much non-truck traffic that the adjacent roads have been left relatively free—and the truck-ers have happily returned to rolling free on the old and now unencumbered roads. Even the high-speed, non-stop driving of the turnpikes has been found by truckers to increase fuel and maintenance costs.

One school of thought has it that railroad piggyback competi-tion, by cutting into all trucking, will affect the toll roads. Mov-ing trailers by piggyback has enjoyed increasing success, especially in New England and on the New York Central's westward runs. Coverdale & Colpitt . . . says, "The railroads are waking up—they're trying to move packaged freight in much faster time than ever before."

Still, most engineers agree that for the long term truck traffic as a percentage of all traffic will continue to grow, and since it pays the biggest tolls it will continue to increase the turnpike revenues.

Already, and despite all talk of changing patterns, most toll roads have done very well indeed. Revenues of the Pennsylvania Turnpike have grown steadily since the end of World War II. The New Jersey Turnpike has run so far ahead of the engineers' estimates of earnings . . . that it has embarrassed the experts nearly as much, though more happily, than the West Virginia Turnpike.

Toll roads are nothing new on the American scene; they had quite a boom in the early nineteenth century. Then they fell into eclipse, with the revival not beginning until 1940, when the Pennsylvania Turnpike began its immensely successful career.

During the war, plans were hatched for a nation-wide high-way system, and the states dreamed up toll road projects to cope with the expected postwar burgeoning of traffic. When peace came, the Maine Turnpike was the first to get going. In 1948 and again in 1949, the Pennsylvania Turnpike financed exten-sions with bond issues. Finally, in 1950, the total volume of toll road bond offering reached $200 million.

In that year, the Jersey Turnpike issue was the biggest single issue, but Oklahoma's Turner Turnpike and the Denver-Boulder road in Colorado also came on the market. The boom was under way, though it petered briefly in 1951 with a mere $35 million supplemental issue in New Jersey.

In 1952, the total offering reached $494 million, for 361 miles of road. Ohio's $326 million issue was the largest up to that time; West Virginia, Oklahoma, and Pennsylvania also floated toll road issues. In the following year, the total reached $1.019 billion—more than all previous years put together. Issues were floated by New York, Maine, and New Jersey—the latter for both the Turnpike and the Garden State Parkway.

The climb continued in 1954, which topped the 1953 total by $500 million. Massachusetts, Connecticut, and Kentucky were newcomers who joined New York, New Jersey, Oklahoma, and Pennsylvania at the toll road trough. Through 1954, toll road bonds had added up to $4.7 billion, for 2,382 miles of pike. Then 1955, on paper, scheduled $4.4 billion, with the single year threatening to equal all that had gone before. It looked huge, but it fizzled, as issue after issue was deferred down to a meager $750 million.

How much of a comeback there may be this year will hang on the effect of the Federal highway bill, plus the same considerations that prevailed last year, sharpened by the record of the few roads that are in trouble.

THE TRUCKING PROBLEM [12]

The average motorist thinks of trucks on the highway as little more than hair-raising hazards. To him, they seem to increase daily in numbers. And he's right; they do.

In fact, the trucking industry has grown to be a tremendous economic giant. It is the second-largest employer in the United States—second only to agriculture—with more than 6 million workers on its payroll. It hauls more than 133 billion ton-miles a year.

[12] From "Where Do Trucks Go from Here?" *Business Week*. p70+. November 22, 1952. Reprinted by special permission of *Business Week*, a McGraw-Hill publication. Copyright 1952 by McGraw-Hill Publishing Company.

Such a vast movement along the nation's highways is obviously a growing problem for the motorist. But it is a great deal
more than that. . . . Highway officials and industry people admit it has created some serious problems for the states, the Federal Government—and for the industry itself.

One reason for this is that the trucking industry is probably
one of the most loosely organized businesses in the United States.
Few other industries know as little about or have as little direct
control over all of their fingers.

There is no central authority, no single data-collecting or co-
ordinating agency to keep track of all of the 9,035,754 trucks
registered in 1951. Only certain interstate carriers, which are
under the economic thumb of the Interstate Commerce Commission, have to report details of their movements. And they add up
only to somewhat over 1 million of all the trucks in use.

Why has such a large industry had so little organization?

In the main it's because trucking, which started out as a
chaotic, catch-as-catch-can business in the early 1900's is still essentially a small-business operation. More than half of the trucks
are owned by individuals who have just one truck.

Up to now the industry has got along very well in this loose-
knit fashion. It has expanded at a terrific rate. Registrations
jumped from a little over 1 million in 1920 to around 4.5 million
by 1940. They crossed the 9 million line last year.

Ton-mileage (a ton of cargo hauled one mile) followed the
same curve upward. Today it is six times the volume of 1920,
far outstripping the rise in vehicle miles. This means bigger
trucks and is important because revenues are determined by ton-
miles and expenses largely by vehicle miles. How important it is
shows up in part in the steady increase in intercity revenues of
common carriers, which rose from under $600 million in 1939
to more than $3 billion in 1950.

A number of things combined to enable the industry to make
these leaps and bounds. Many of them are inherent in the truck
itself. Highly important has been the truck's flexibility. It can
go anywhere, anytime. To the shipper this means faster service
and shorter transit time—which in turn means less handling of
cargo and less inventory the shipper has to keep on hand.

Then, too, the truck is extremely adaptable cargowise. It can carry anything from less-than-carload, small package goods to bulk cargo like steel, lumber, ore. It can transport commodities that other forms of transportation can't, or don't, handle.

Besides this, the trend toward decentralization of industry has put many plants in spots where they have to depend entirely on trucks. Also, the very economics of the trucking business may well have fostered growth to some extent.

Relatively, you don't need very much capital to set yourself up in trucking—and return on investment is fairly high, even though profit margins are essentially low. Companies have no initial investment in their rights of way, the highways.

Under these and other more-or-less favorable conditions, the trucking industry tumbled into maturity. And that very development has brought the industry face to face with the hard fact that it can no longer fall over its feet like a puppy. Its size and importance demand that as a whole it be brought under some kind of internal and external discipline comparable to that required by other transportation lifelines when they came of age. . . .

Kinds of Trucking

Typical of the loose-jointed anatomy of the industry is the fact that not everybody agrees on just what should properly be called the trucking industry. Some would limit it to the for-hire carriers—a small segment. That leaves out close to 2.5 million farmer-owned and operated trucks, about 300,000 trucks operated by Federal, state, and local governments, and around 4.5 million private carriers that are owned by stores, distributors, manufacturers, and the like to transport their own goods—the largest single group.

For its purposes ICC [Interstate Commerce Commission] breaks the for-hires down into three groups: contract, exempt, and common carriers.

Last year something under three thousand contract carriers were subject to ICC control. These are the ones that make specific contracts with individual shippers to carry their freight in interstate commerce. A contract carrier must get an operating permit from ICC; he doesn't have to file specific rates, but must report a schedule of minimum rates.

The exempt carriers also do business interstate, but they are subject only to ICC safety regulations. They include special-service trucks, such as newspaper delivery trucks, trucks owned and operated by co-ops, and carriers that haul agricultural commodities and fish. There are about twice as many exempt carriers as contract and common carriers combined.

The common carriers are the trucks that haul general freight. They include moving vans, tank trucks, automobile carriers. There are about eight times as many common as contract carriers. Their rates, routes, and sometimes commodities carried are set up by ICC. They are the ones that are actually engaged in the transportation business.

Bearing Down

Over the years sizes and weights of these trucks have been increasing steadily. Twenty years ago about five trucks in one hundred had axle weights of more than 18,000 pounds; today ten in one hundred have, according to the Bureau of Public Roads.

All the while trucks have been getting bigger and heavier, the nation's roads have been rapidly deteriorating. A lot of the blame has been shoved on the trucks. The railroads, and sometimes the public, scream that the truckers are not paying a fair share of the costs. The truckers say they are. Nobody can prove it either way.

In the middle are the states. Highways cost money, and it is largely the states' responsibility to find ways and means—through license and registration fees, gasoline taxes, and other levies. Their problem is to apportion the costs among all highway users so that each group of vehicles pays its fair share.

There has been a growing conviction on the part of the states, and the public, that the heavy trucks are in large part responsible for the breaking up of highways, and that therefore they should carry a bigger share of the tax load. This has led to another, graduated highway-use tax for trucks, based on weight and mileage.

Truckers are fighting the weight-distance principle tooth and nail, and will continue to do so. They insist that such a tax is unfair, and that it is uneconomical for the states to administer. They also claim that it creates highway barriers between states and is weakening the foundations of reciprocity, a principle they are jealously guarding.

Nine states now have specific taxes based on weight-distance on out-of-state trucks. An indication of what lies ahead came ... in Oregon, where the public voted overwhelmingly to continue and to boost that state's weight-distance levy. More such crackdowns are sure to follow.

Just how much damage to the roads is caused by weight, and just where the breaking point comes has yet to be conclusively proved. Actually, the load carried on a single axle, rather than gross weight, is the chief determining factor.

In 1949 the Highway Research Board of the National Research Council conducted a six-month, controlled-traffic road test in Maryland to see what the effects of four different axle loads would be on a concrete pavement. The results of this test have been much publicized—to prove vastly different views. Nearly everyone agrees, however that the results were nowhere near conclusive. But it is a step in the direction of finding a practical answer to the trucks' relationship to the over-all traffic and highway problem.

Whatever such tests may prove, one thing is certain: The trucking industry can look forward to a heavier tax load for some time to come.

Tightening Up

All forty-eight states today have laws that limit the weight, number of axles, and, in most cases, length of trucks that travel on its roads. However, these limits are anything but uniform; they vary all over the lot.

This lack of uniformity is one of the biggest single problems the industry has to wrestle with. Obviously there never could be complete uniformity across the country. That's because of regional differences in geography and traffic conditions. But the truckers are devoting a great deal of time and effort to working out the problem with the states—to ward off the bogeyman of Federal intervention.

Increasing concern of the Federal Government with the relationship of the trucking industry to over-all transportation policy, too, raises the question of whether tighter Federal control of the industry is at hand. There are some signs of it right now. ICC approval is required for any mergers or consolidations, or other major transactions involving shifts in control. In the past when the industry was growing so fast and routes were being expanded steadily, such acquisitions were processed as a matter of routine. In the last year or so, however, ICC has been giving such applications much closer scrutiny. The whole process of expansion by acquisition is getting much more complicated and is being made more difficult.

TRUCKS, TRAILERS, AND TURNPIKES [13]

Fifty years of truck building and operating have underscored a basic economic fact: As the size and weight of trucks increase, operating costs per unit shrink.

Fifty years of road building and use have given rise to a belief generally accepted by the public (though still hotly debated by engineers and truckmen): As loads placed on pavements and bridges increase, their building and upkeep costs shoot up.

But half a century has not provided answers to these questions:

How big can trucks get before the law of diminishing returns rules out further growth?

Exactly what is the correlation between truck weights and road costs?

There's no doubt that it is becoming increasingly important to find the answers. There are more than 9 million trucks on the highway today. By 1975 the President's Materials Policy Commission predicts there will be more than twice that number. Recently, the whole issue has been blurred by the dust and noise of

[13] From "Nailing Down the Facts in the Truck Issue." *Business Week.* p 106-8. March 7, 1953. Reprinted by special permission of *Business Week,* a McGraw-Hill publication. Copyright 1953 by McGraw-Hill Publishing Company.

a public relations battle between the truckers and the railroads. This has centered on the fact that trucks use publicly paid and maintained facilities, for which they pay only part of the cost, while the railroads must build and maintain their own rights of way.

But further behind the scenes, quieter—and probably more far-reaching—tests are taking shape. Truckers, manufacturers of paving materials, and the engineers and contractors who build the roads, are taking part in scientific projects aimed at determining just what damage—if any—a properly built and weighted truck will do to a properly built road. It's undeniable that a poorly built road will break up under truck pounding, but it will also crumble under less heavy traffic. How much can a soundly constructed road stand? And just what is a properly built road?

That problem must be solved before any sensible figures can be obtained as to what trucks are costing and will cost the public for road building and maintenance. It gets into some highly technical matters: How should the sub-base of a road be compacted, and what should it consist of? Should the main part of the road be concrete, oil-based, asphalt, or something else? What kind of wearing surface should the road have?

There are no definitive findings yet. But engineers are working hard—in the laboratories, through test applications on state roads, and by using specially built road sections.

One research program that should uncover some fundamental facts of truck and highway construction has been launched by the Highway Research Board of the National Academy of Science, which works closely with the Bureau of Public Roads. The board has mapped out a long-range study to find out what weights and sizes of trucks can be balanced with highways of appropriate capacities to produce the lowest possible costs for truck transport. The board will work through a committee made up of men from various phases of trucking, highway officials, and representatives of government agencies.

The committee will kick off by probing into the doings of truck companies and users. It will analyze such matters as packaging procedures, total tonnages, product densities, to work out the optimum payload for goods most frequently shipped. Mean-

while, the committee will also be sifting through questionnaires
returned by motor carriers. They'll be toting up operating costs
of truck combinations from 35,000 pounds up.

Regardless of what the curve of operating costs in relation
to gross weight will plot, however, one thing is certain: It will be
meaningless until it is crossed by another curve showing road
construction and maintenance costs.

Something is being done about that, too. Lately highway
pavements have come in for some serious testing, and they are
scheduled for a lot more. One study, the Maryland Road Test,
completed . . . [in 1952] has lost much of its engineering significance through its involvement in the struggle for shipping dollars
between eastern truckers and railroaders.

In the Maryland test, four loadings—ranging from 18,000
pounds to 44,800 pounds—were used, on single and tandem
axles. Visitors were permitted, with the result that anti-truckers
got a chance to make capital of pictures showing damage. The
final report on the test showed that road breakdown occurred
where the truck loads were heavy. But these road sections also
had poor subgrades—and the effects could not be disentangled.

Meanwhile, engineers have been busy designing more tests.
. . . In Iowa, a highway research board set up by the legislature in
1949 is considering a permanent test track. The plan calls for
a circular track on which many kinds of roads could be built,
studied, and dismantled. To eliminate human error, test trucks
would be driverless, steered by rods riding on guide rails.

The biggest test of all is planned by the American Association
of State Highway Officials. The test, which will cost an estimated
$4 million, will probably take place in Illinois, and will be ad-
ministered by the Highway Research Board. It will test both
Portland cement concrete and asphaltic concrete. The study's aim
will be to develop criteria to be used in:

Design and construction of new pavements, and maintenance
and improvement of existing roads.

Writing of laws covering weight limits and taxes for highway
users.

The controversy between asphaltic concrete and Portland
cement concrete is a sharp one, with millions of dollars at stake.

Hardly a major highway is built without a skirmish between partisans of the two materials. Both sides are vying eagerly for the recent rush of big toll roads and throughways. Cement wins in one state, asphalt in another.

The bitterness and ramifications of this fight were indicated in Ohio recently when a court referee found that the Ohio Turnpike Commission had exercised "an abuse of discretion" in deciding to accept bids only for Portland cement materials for its toll road across northern Ohio.

THE CASE AGAINST TRUCKS [14]

If you're an observant motorist, you may sometimes wonder why you encounter so many huge trucks, obviously of the long-distance type, lumbering along out-of-the-way roads. You may also occasionally notice red flags flying from some gasoline stations and roadside diners along main highways which seem free from unusual dangers. You may even pass a man peering intently through field glasses and making mysterious motions with his left arm. These peculiar doings are symbols of the most fantastic battle of wits on the highways since the rumrunning era. It is practically nation-wide, and in some sections it includes such melodramatic touches as spies and counterespionage, elaborate warning networks, high-speed chases, ambushes, bribery and even hints of sudden death.

The contest is between trucks loaded beyond legal limits and state officials who charge that such vehicles endanger lives and wreck our roads. Many of the gigantic trucks meandering over side roads miles off the routes to main shipping centers are trying to evade traps set by the officials. The red flags are signals warning that state weight inspectors are operating nearby. The man with the field glasses may be a spy who has spotted a mobile weighing crew lying in ambush, and the pumping motion of his left arm is the truck drivers' universal code for "Danger ahead!"

[14] From "Are Trucks Destroying Our Highways?" by David G. Wittels, free-lance writer. *Saturday Evening Post.* 223:19-21+. September 16, 1950. Reprinted by permission.

On a sunny afternoon early this summer such a spotter was stationed on U S 1, the main highway between New England and Florida. He was partly hidden by a clump of bushes alongside the road, atop a rise a few miles south of Baltimore. Most of the trucks he signaled kept right on going, merely blinking their rear lights as they passed. That's the truck drivers' way of acknowledging a signal and saying "Thanks, pal." These trucks were "cream puffs"—lightly or at least legally loaded—and so had nothing to fear from the inspection station set up a mile southward.

But about every tenth long-distance truck hissed in vehement protest as its driver pumped the air brakes to bring the mammoth vehicle to a halt. Apparently those drivers knew they were overloaded. For them the ambush up ahead meant delay, fines and maybe jail sentences.

Some of these pulled over to the side of the road and smoked or went to sleep, waiting until the weighing crew would go away. Some turned back to alternate roads which would detour them around the ambush. The first few stopped at the nearest telephones to flash warnings to Baltimore and Washington, and even as far north and south as Philadelphia and Richmond. Sometimes truck centers more than one hundred miles away get such warnings within ten minutes after a trap is set. . . .

The spying, evasive tactics and other shenanigans are used only by the flagrant and habitual violators. But underlying the cops-and-robbers scenes is a combat which, while less visibly spectacular, is one of the bitterest and most significant business wars being waged in this country today. Literally billions of dollars are involved. The main battles are being fought in state legislatures and in Congress.

Four groups are concerned in this brawl. On one side is the burgeoning trucking industry, which in the past few years has leaped from comparative insignificance to seriously challenge the railroads for the nation's freight-carrying business. It is battling to get limits raised so that it can roll even huger trucks and carry even heavier loads. Though a comparatively young industry, the truckers are strongly organized and have an ample war chest.

They operate powerful lobbies in most of the states and in Washington.

Arrayed against the truckers are rather strange teammates. In the forefront are state and Federal highway officials, trying to lower the weight limits or at least hold the line. Backing them up, but operating more or less backstage, are the railroads. Those two groups are odd bedfellows, because the highway officials' motive is to save and improve the roads; and the better the roads the more they can lure passengers out of trains into automobiles and buses.

But the railroads right now are worrying about the immediate threat to their freight business, which generally is more profitable than passenger trade. They are frightened by the fact that the big trucks already have grabbed more than one fourth of the long-haul freight revenues, currently totaling about $10 billion a year. Therefore they are applying terrific political pressure and firing expensive propaganda guns.

The fourth group is most aptly described by the cartoonists' classical figure of a meek, bewildered little gent. He is the tax-payer; particularly, in this case, the motorist. As usual, he is hardly aware that his wallet is one of the stakes.

The tax money involved is astronomical. In the past fifty years $60 billion have been spent on construction and maintenance of our 3.3 million miles of roads and streets. . . . But apparently that isn't enough. The United States Bureau of Public Roads estimates that "to bring all roads and streets up to adequate standards would require the expenditure of $60 billion." The bureau also warns that, at the present rate, in six years "only 56 per cent of the high-type roads now in use will be in usable shape. This will be the status despite the reconstruction programmed between now and them." In other words, the main highways are breaking up faster than we're building or repairing them.

What caused this horrible mess? A few extremists blame it all on the big trucks. Highway officials don't make any such charge; they say that, of course, age, weather and the lack of new construction and proper maintenance during the war years had a lot to do with it. But they do blame giant trucks for a large

part of the wreckage. . . . [United States Commissioner of Public
Roads Thomas H. MacDonald] points to a thirty-mile stretch of
concrete highway in Missouri which was "in excellent condition"
until the main stream of Chicago-St. Louis traffic was temporarily
routed over it. After up to 1500 trucks per day pounded it for
six months, it was so broken up that a makeshift patching job
cost $150,000.

A county road in northeastern Maryland was rated "in good
shape" when floods on a main highway forced it to bear a heavy
traffic of huge trucks for twenty-four hours. At the end of those
twenty-four hours this road was "all but demolished." In another
part of Maryland, long-distance trucks were detoured over State
Road 12 while their usual route was being repaired. Engineers
had figured the road should last another ten years. After a couple
of months of heavy truck traffic, it was "broken to bits."

There is a road in Pennsylvania which bears heavy truck traffic for part of its length. After that nearly all trucks swing onto
a turnpike. Pennsylvania officials claim the stretch used by heavy
trucks costs fourteen times as much per mile to maintain as the
section used almost solely by passenger cars and light local trucks.

Though the trucking industry denies that legally weighted
trucks cause more than reasonable wear and tear to the roads, it
indirectly admits that overloaded rigs are a menace. Without
mentioning damage to roads, the American Trucking Associations, Incorporated, spokesman for the industry, "vigorously and
unqualifiedly condemns the practice of violations of state truck-
weight laws by anyone."

The joker is that some trucking firms whose executives most
piously deplore such practices are among the worst offenders.
That doesn't mean that most firms deliberately flout the law;
some even make it a firing offense to overload a truck. But Maryland files show that out of sixty-three firms, ranging in size from
one truck to one thousand two hundred, which operate in or
through that state, eight of the biggest are habitual violators. . . .
[One] company's trucks were nabbed more than one hundred
times during a period when Maryland had only a few inspectors
and figured it was catching less than 10 per cent of the violators.

Michigan, also operating with limited forces, caught one firm 177 times. A survey in Illinois found 27 per cent of the trucks stopped overweight; spot checks in Indiana and Oklahoma each indicated 35 per cent, and a test in Nebraska revealed half the biggest trucks to be overloaded. Hence the nation-wide cops-and-robbers game on the highways.

Game is not an inapt term, despite the seriousness underlying it. This is because no state has enough crews to guard all roads at all times, and even if it were possible, stopping all trucks for inspection would jam traffic and unfairly penalize honest truckers. Therefore fixed weighing stations are rarely manned more than a couple of hours at a time, and mobile crews almost never stay at one spot more than an hour. The result is a combination of guessing game and hide-and-seek, with overloaded truckers trying to get advance clues as to when and where the weighers are in action, and the officials staggering hours and jumping their mobile crews from road to road to keep the truckers from guessing right. . . .

The story of how Maryland got involved in such shenanigans is typical of the more than two dozen states currently engaged in or preparing for intensified enforcement. Most states began worrying about what trucks were doing to their roads shortly after World War I. Trucks were still comparative midgets then, but they had solid tires which obviously were breaking up the rather weak roads of that period. Two things happened almost simultaneously; the solid tires were quickly legislated off the highways, and the nation began its greatest era of road building, which lasted into the early thirties. The new roads were stronger, and the states relaxed.

The current problem sneaked up on them. In the last few years the number, size and weight of trucks have increased fantastically. The number practically doubled in about ten years, until today nearly 8.5 million trucks are operating. The motorist who has nightmares about being surrounded by galloping, behemothlike trucks isn't entirely dreaming. A truck manufacturer has estimated that 17 per cent of all vehicles today are trucks. On the basis of usage of the roads, their incidence is even higher. A survey by the United States Bureau of Public Roads in 1948

showed that 25 per cent of the traffic on main highways, outside
cities, consisted of trucks. And a New Jersey official says that one
out of every three vehicles on the main highways in his state is
a truck.

But the number doesn't frighten the officials; they accept that
as a necessary part of our modern economy. It's the increasing
weight that gives them the horrors. There are several ways of
figuring truck weights. One favored by engineers is by the load
on each axle. The percentage of trucks hammering the roads
with eleven tons or more per axle has increased tenfold in the
past few years. A more familiar gauge is the over-all weight.
The ratio of trucks weighing twenty-five tons or more has gone
up twelve times. Most states now allow much more than twenty-
five tons, and in at least one the truckers are trying to get that
raised to seventy tons.

But highway officials insist the roads weren't built to take
such loads. They point out that even most of our main highways
were built when engineers envisioned loads of only nine tons per
axle. In addition, much of the network is between twenty and
thirty years old, less able than ever to take a battering from
overloads.

Maryland awoke with a start in the winter of 1948-49. That
was a very bad winter for roads. Heavy frosts followed by sudden thaws played particular hob with them. Soon extensive symp-
toms of two types of weakening appeared. One is descriptively
known as "frost boils" and occurs only on so-called flexible roads
—that is, macadam. A section as much as thirty-six inches in
diameter, and once in a great while the whole width of the road,
may bulge up as much as ten or twelve inches. Even a lightly
loaded truck or a heavy car may crumble that. The second and
more expensive type occurs in concrete highways and is known
as "pumping." Concrete roads aren't solid ribbons, but consist of
sections, or slabs, separated by tarlike substances. Water seeping
between or under those slabs turns the soil on which the slabs
rest into mud. Monstrous trucks pounding onto the slabs can
cause them to tilt or rock, creating a pumping action. Highway
officials insist that this happens often. Trucking leaders claim
that is exaggerated, but an experienced truck driver told this

writer, "I've seen slabs tilt when I hit them, and the mud squirted out like a fountain." As a result, the soil base becomes uneven and pocked; and the slabs are ready to crack and crumble under the onslaught of other heavy trucks.

Maryland's weight law, permitting axle loads of 22,400 pounds each and an over-all weight of thirty-four tons, is liberal compared with most. But it also permits the State Roads Commission to lower the limits in emergencies. In this bad winter the limit was lowered to nine tons per axle on a few miles of the 16,600 miles of state and county roads. Since only several stretches were involved, it was easy to police them—even with a few part-time crews. The officials got a shock. They discovered that not only were most big trucks ignoring the emergency limit, but many were exceeding the top limit.

But even while these officials were worrying about their roads that bad winter, the trucking industry started a drive for even heavier loads. It introduced a bill into the legislature to raise the limit to forty-five tons. That made Robert M. Reindollar, chairman of the State Roads Commission, fighting mad. . . . He got even madder when he asked a leader of the trucking industry why he hadn't been consulted on the bill. According to Reindollar, the trucking executive replied: "Oh, we don't care what the road commission thinks. We've got the legislature in our pocket."

The bill sailed through the legislature as predicted. Reindollar countered as best he could by ordering the still-existing law strictly enforced. . . . In six months, with only five crews operating, 1,900 trucks were caught overloaded.

At the last minute Governor William Preston Lane, Jr. killed the bill. "Neither the roads nor the bridges in Maryland," his veto message said, "have been designed to carry burdens of this tremendous weight. Such an increase . . . not only would jeopardize (them) but would greatly increase the cost of future construction." . . .

So far the habitual violators do not seem much chastened by Maryland's drive, or by the recent, current or planned campaigns in . . . other states. . . . The flagrant violations are continuing because the fines, ranging from $10 to $200, are small compared to potential profits from overloading. The present odds in most states are that the truck won't be caught, and it has been estimated that a big truck overloaded 10,000 pounds each trip can pile up extra gross revenue of $12,500 a year. There is a wry sequel to the story of the overweight truck which broke down a $100,000 bridge in New Jersey. The fine for this was $131. But motorists who stopped to rubberneck at the wreckage were fined $156 for illegal parking. . . .

On the major battle of whether legal loads damage roads, and whether limits should be increased, the trucking industry has interesting arguments. Its main defenses, paraphrased, run somewhat like this: (1) the highways are not wearing out faster than should be expected; (2) if they are, the fault is bad weather and bad engineering; (3) the trucks are paying for any damage by exorbitant taxes.

The question of whether the big trucks pay their fair share, in license fees, gasoline taxes and other levies, is hotly debated. . . . Briefly, the truckers claim they are paying more than their fair share; the other side charges that the truckers are getting a free ride at the expense of private motorists and taxpayers in general.

Still another argument by the truckers is that conflicting state laws have them so confused and bewildered that they practically can't help breaking the law. A truck of legal length and weight in New York, headed for Florida, could be in trouble the moment it left New York. In New Jersey it would be five feet too long; in Pennsylvania it would be both overlong and overweight. It would become legal again in Maryland, but upon entering the District of Columbia it would be overweight. In Virginia and North Carolina it could be fined for overlength and overweight. In South Carolina it would be O.K. as to length but wrong as to weight; in Georgia it would be illegal both ways, and in Florida it would be more than two tons overweight on its rear tractor axles even though the gross weight of the rig was within the legal over-all weight limit.

This argument is incontrovertibly true. The catch is that the American Association of State Highway Officials has offered a model code to standardize truck sizes and fix weight limits at nine tons per axle or an over-all weight of thirty-four tons. The truckers are battling this in every state legislature in which it has been introduced.

To objective observers whom this writer interviewed, the best argument in favor of the truckers is simply the fact that they have become an important, essential part of the modern economy. Therefore the argument as to whether, on a strict bookkeeping basis, they pay a pro-rata share of highway costs becomes partly beside the point. A number of other essential industries get subsidies, hidden or otherwise. The question narrows to (a) how much of the multibillion-dollar highways bill should rightly be charged to the trucks and (b) how huge can they be allowed to get without utterly ruining the roads.

The first part probably will never be fully settled. The second part is now being doubly tested in Maryland. When Governor Lane vetoed the bill to raise limits to 90,000 pounds, he also appointed a committee headed by Albert S. Gordon, executive secretary of the State Roads Commission. "Get the facts," he said, "so you can tell the 1951 legislature what would be a fair law all around." . . .

A 1.1-mile stretch of modern concrete highway on U S 301, in Maryland, was chosen as the guinea pig. Since June of this year trucks have been pounding over that road night and day. The stretch was divided into four approximately equal parts, to be hammered by trucks with loads ranging from 18,000 to 44,800 pounds per axle. Truck manufacturers donated the trucks, tiremakers the tires, oil companies the gasoline and lubricants. The . . . round-the-clock ordeal is to continue for six months, but the full findings probably won't be ready for a year.

The verdict from this test, if it works out according to highway officials' expectations, may result in better roads and—just perhaps—a decrease in the average motorists' taxes. However it turns out, it probably will have tremendous effect on the freight-transportation pattern throughout the country. [The test was inconclusive. See preceding article, "Trucks, Trailers, and Turnpikes," and "Highway Engineering," in Section III, below.—Ed.]

THE CASE FOR TRUCKS [15]

Road officials, tax officials, automotive outfits, writers, anyone who needs a convenient whipping boy for traffic annoyances has it ready-made in the trucks and trailers. They're too big and too numerous to be overlooked. And in our nation of car drivers obliged to share the rights of way with commercial vehicles, the popular mind seems too ready to find plausibility in the most far-fetched arguments against the big "intruders."

During 1950, for example, three national magazines . . . assailed trucks as a threat to the nation's roads. . . . Approximately the same arguments, and even a few of the same facts and episodes, figured in all three publications. How explain a coincidence that looks remarkably like a gang-up?

The answer of course is that editors are all too human, and share the irrational spleens of their readers. This makes them easy targets for anti-truck propaganda with a special interest in the everlasting competition for the transport dollar. Having been discommoded at one time or another, perhaps while out for a Sunday drive, by a line of oversized vehicles hauling livestock or gasoline, logs or refrigerated fish, an indictment of trucks reaching their desks finds them receptive and, alas, uncritical.

Neither the editor nor the reader stops to consider that highways, from time immemorial, have been primarily arteries of trade. If there is an "intruder" on the roads, it is more likely to be the individual motorist. To hound trucks from the highways on any pretext, to make existence onerous for the trucking industry, makes about as much sense as barring city streets to vehicular traffic because it infringes on the comfort of pedestrians.

The trucking population of our roads has grown steadily, from some 300,000 during the First World War to some 8 million today. Thirteen per cent of the nation's freight is hauled by motorized vehicles as against 4 per cent thirty years ago. But this expansion has not been accidental or arbitrary. It has come

[15] From "In Defense of Trucks" by John S. Worley, late head of the Department of Transportation Engineering, University of Michigan. *American Mercury.* 73:112-18. November 1951. Copyright 1951 by American Mercury Magazine, Inc. Reprinted by permission.

as a direct response to economic imperatives. The growth reflects, and in turn accelerates, an American way of life in which the small town, in the heart of the continent and off the chartered railway tracks, expects and gets, as a matter of course, the multifarious products of our farms and factories from all parts of the country.

The truck, unlike the railroad freighter, can go wherever there is a road and often where there isn't any. It has been rightly described as "tailor-made," in the sense that it can be designed for the special needs of any area, any product, any load. This, plus the flexibility of trucking time schedules, has given transportation a new dimension of efficiency. The truck, for instance, has become the mainstay of small businesses which cannot afford to buy their supplies in carloads.

As American industry is increasingly decentralized and deployed to smaller communities, in effect breaking out of the former straitjacket of the rail network, its dependence on trucking increases correspondingly. In fact, trucks provide indispensable links between industry and rail terminals at one end, between rail terminals and destination at the other end. Retailers, now able to replenish their stocks daily and thus avoid costly inventories and warehousing, relish this new freedom made possible by truck deliveries. Motorized transportation, in short, has become a vital element in the national economy and one for which there can be no substitute.

It has been calculated that nearly 15 per cent of all jobs in the country—one in every seven—is provided by the trucking industry. This sounds excessive at first, until we realize that there are over 5 million truck drivers, and nearly 1 million maintenance men; that it takes 1.5 million oil refinery workers to fuel the trucks, while millions more are engaged in all aspects of manufacture, maintenance, sales and supplies for the automotive carriers.

If the individual driver were more conscious of these realities, he might be a bit more forbearing on the issue of roads "infested" by trucks. He would then comprehend that his everyday existence, from the fresh food on his table to the variety of goods in his local emporium, is intimately bound up with that "infestation."

The three magazine articles I mentioned built their case against trucks around episodes of violation of maximum weight laws. They told tales—mostly the same tales, as if pulled out of the same files—about truck drivers who sneak through back roads to evade weight inspectors, or connive with gas-station "spotters" to foil the law. Admittedly this made flamboyant reading. Yet to condemn an entire essential industry for the sins of its lawless brethren is as unreasonable as condemning the entire population of a town by describing a few of its more dissolute characters. . . .

More conscientious checking would have revealed that the offending truckers are a tiny minority; that some of the violations are due to the chaos of conflicting state regulations which sometimes make the law-abiding trucker in forty-seven states a lawbreaker in the forty-eighth; that perfectly legal loads are often turned illegal by a sheer accident, such as a rain that adds tons to the original freight. It would reveal, more importantly, that the trucking industry itself combats the minority of willful violators and has, in addition, long been seeking uniform laws to supersede the present nightmare of contradictions.

That the self-interest of competitors, meaning in this case the railroads, plays a part in churning up anti-truck sentiment is understandable and not in itself reprehensible. Though they are carrying about twice as much freight tonnage as in the boom year of 1929, they cannot be expected to remain indifferent to the challenge of motorized haulage. . . .

The late Joseph B. Eastman, then head of the Office of Defense Transportation, was . . . explicit in discussing the attacks on trucking:

> Unfortunately, the situation has been affected, at times to a controlling extent, by a factor which has nothing to do with the protection of the public safety or the conservation of highways, and that is the desire of the railroads to limit or embarrass the competition which they encounter from motor trucks or buses. The railroads and their employees, who are powerful politically, have been extremely active in seeking state restrictions upon the size and weight of motor vehicles for this purpose and in opposing Federal remedial legislation.

The advent of every new industry has always seemed to the older competitors an invasion of their vested rights. It is the *success* of so much of the railroad propaganda that concerns me here. The annoyance of the individual driver with trucks on the highways, his failure to visualize the extreme importance of the functions performed by the "intruder," provides a fertile soil for those with a dollar-and-cents stake in planting disinformation about the motorized carrier. And the sowing, of course, is prodigious in scale. Besides the large railroads, each with its own public-relations department, there is the Association of American Railroads; there are state and regional railroad organizations; there are the Railroad Brotherhoods. And not one of them has any affection for Cinderella.

Then there are the organizations of, by and for the individual motorists, and in the first place the American Automobile Association. The truck, looking so huge on the driver's horizon, is a natural and almost inescapable target of their ministrations. . . . In shifting upon truckers as large a part as possible of the blame for wear and tear of roads, of the costs of highway building and maintenance, such organizations seem to speak with the powerful voice of the people.

This is not the place for a technical discussion of the causes of the manifold ailments inherent in roads. Suffice that heavy loads are the least of them. The average man, and that includes the average legislator, does not understand that the aggregate weight of a loaded vehicle is not the sole or determining factor. What matters is the number of wheels and the amount of air in each tire. A "light" vehicle on four wheels may exert more pressure than a heavy one on ten wheels. Though trucks are barred from the famous Merritt Parkway in Connecticut, large segments of it have suffered damage; but a parallel truck road is by contrast in first-rate shape. The condition of a road is determined by how well it is built in the first place, the nature of its bed, the efficiency of its maintenance.

I can attest, as a transportation engineer, that the weight of traffic units is minor in the total equation of road health. The tendency of laymen to attribute highway deterioration to the "heavy" vehicles is, in the last analysis due to an optical illusion. The real culprits of road wear, in ninety-nine cases out of a hundred, are the nature of the subsoil, the quality of the construction, the negligence of maintenance crews. But the truck is the one tangible scapegoat. Moreover, there is an amazing amount of exaggeration with respect to the condition of our nation's highways. Testifying on this matter before a Senate subcommittee last year, I declared:

> Recently there have been articles and statements regarding the dilapidated condition of our roads and streets claiming that this alleged condition has been caused by heavy loads. During the last four years, I have given special attention to this subject, which included inspection of many miles of highways in many states.
>
> I found that our roads and streets were not in the condition reported. I found that both functionally and physically they were in a condition equal to or better than the average of our industrial plants. Wherever there was evidence of faulting in the pavement, it was due to neglected maintenance and not heavy trucks.

The trucking industry, to make matters worse for the much-maligned truckman, is inherently incapable of effective rebuttal to . . . pressure-group accusations. Though a gigantic business in the aggregate, it is composed of an enormous number of little businesses, tens of thousands of them possessing just one truck. About 85 per cent of all trucks and trailers in the hauling trade are in fleets of less than eight vehicles. In confronting the powerful railway organization, the AAA, the Federal and local highway agencies, they are in effect a dispersed and impotent group of little men. In the last few years true enough, a few of them have begun to "talk back." But their voice is still just a whisper.

I do not wish to imply that the industry is without faults or sins—that could scarcely be said of any enterprise of this magnitude, particularly one that is relatively young and not yet fully adjusted. Its organization and leading companies acknowledge the need for sound, scientific ceilings on size and weight of trucks on a uniform nation-wide basis. While fighting unfair and discriminatory regulations and imposts in forty-eight legislatures, they have shown themselves ready to bear an equitable portion of the costs of maintaining and extending the national highway system.

IF WAR SHOULD COME [16]

On the morning of July 7, 1919, a strange convoy chugged down Washington's Pennsylvania Avenue, passed the White House and bravely headed west. It consisted of sixty World War I trucks and twenty touring cars dressed with flags and Army recruiting posters. Proudly perched beside one driver was a young officer named Dwight D. Eisenhower.

Sixty-three days, 3,000 miles, and some 1,900 breakdowns later the bedraggled entourage limped into San Francisco. Behind it was strewn a nightmare of hardships and delay. Dust had stalled engines and mud had mired both men and machines. In the Salt Lake Desert the caravan made only two miles in twenty-four hours with the soldiers pulling the trucks over the sand by rope.

Despite such frustrations this first cross-country convoy proved the vital need for an adequate system of highways for the defense and economic well-being of the country.

During the recent Korean War, several truckloads of desperately needed material zoomed 2,500 road miles from Columbus, Ohio, to shipside in San Francisco within five days. Mountains of industrial goods daily criss-cross the country's highways on fast, tight schedules. Does this mean our roads are now adequate for all needs of national defense?

Unfortunately, no. Military experts point out that these peacetime feats are accomplished without harassment from the enemy and the displacement of hundreds of thousands of civilians that must be expected in a concerted attack.

"Today's crucial national defense needs," says Major General Paul F. Yount, Chief of Transportation of the United States Army, "lie in improving to modern standards the forty-thousand-mile Interstate Highway System. This vital network must be able to handle the tremendous volume and weight of military, industrial, and civilian traffic that will flood our arterial highways in the event of a national emergency."

[16] From "Highways in National Defense" by Jay Dugan, writer and advertising executive. *Freedom of the American Road.* Ford Motor Company. 3000 Schaefer Road. Dearborn, Michigan. 1956. p 18. Reprinted by permission.

The ability to wage modern warfare, he said, is gauged by the number and speed of a nation's wheels. The great flexibility of highway transport makes this medium loom ever larger in military planning. Even in peacetime 1954, he pointed out, more than 8 million tons of military freight moved over America's highways on government bills of lading.

In wartime at least 70 million people might have to be evacuated from cities. "In the case of an atomic attack on our key cities, the road net must permit quick evacuation of target areas, mobilization of defense forces, and maintenance of every essential function. But the present highway system in critical areas would be the breeder of a deadly congestion within hours of an attack." This from the young officer of the 1919 convoy, speaking now as President of the United States.

Most of the present interstate highways were designed for traffic peaks that were passed eight years ago. In the event of war large scale military movements alone would pose serious capacity problems.

Suppose, for instance, it were necessary for a single armored division to move quickly cross-country. The 3,200 vehicles of the division strung out in single file, since much of the system is one-lane in each direction, would stretch some twenty miles. How long would it take this convoy to reach San Francisco from Washington?

Perhaps it would never get there intact. One reason is the condition of the bridges. Of the 12,600 in the Interstate System, more than 700 are below tolerable strength standards. About 100 structures have clearances too low or too narrow to accommodate the combat vehicles.

If a major city on the route had suffered a direct A-bomb hit, the division's progress would be seriously hampered or stopped. Most mileage on the system today leads directly into the heart of cities. Only a small fraction consists of controlled or limited-access highways. Through traffic on about 90 per cent of the mileage is delayed and hampered by intersecting roads and private driveways.

"We must build modern arterial limited-access highways free of the restrictions that prevent efficient and safe transportation," said General Yount. "Improvement of the 2,300 miles recently added to the interstate system should mostly take the form of circumferential routes around population centers. And it is of major importance that wherever traffic volume is high, the 40,000 miles should have limited and controlled access."

In what ways do our normal peacetime highway needs differ from those of defense?

"In the present concept, they don't," says General Yount. "Our wartime potential is only an extension of our peacetime resources. The same improved highway system that would best serve our economic welfare in time of peace would also serve our defense with maximum efficiency in time of war."

III. THE ROAD AHEAD

EDITOR'S INTRODUCTION

Roads are like schools. Everyone knows they are necessary and desirable, but controversy has raged for centuries over who should foot the bill. Should they be maintained by the state at public expense, free to all, or should their costs be charged only to those who use them? In America the solution to both problems has been virtually the same. Basic roads and basic schools are provided from general funds for the general welfare, for not even the pedestrian or the celibate can say he receives no benefit. Both enjoy the goods and services and progress that come by road, and both enjoy the high standards of living and culture that only an educated people can maintain.

But while all enjoy the advantages of roads and schools, each man's contribution toward their maintenance is measured to some extent by the actual use he makes of them. Thus for higher education we charge tuition, and for the improvement of roads we have user taxes—and here the analogy ends. No state would dream of charging an exceptionally bright student (or an exceptionally dull one) for his added demands on the teacher, but dispute has endured for years over the relative price to be paid for the use of roads by various classes of vehicles. The danger to our highway system inherent in such controversy—described by Theodore H. White in the first article that follows—is probably greater than the dangers of excessive weight, misuse, and neglect combined, and the dangers latent in other areas of discord are equally grave.

Despite nation-wide differences of opinion, however—and Samuel W. Taylor, in "The Battle For Highways—In California" shows how they seep down to the smallest political subdivision of a state—the very passage of the Federal-Aid Highway and Highway Revenue Acts of 1956 (Public Law 627) demonstrates that the country is willing to pay for the roads our economy and defense require. Between the defeat of the 1955 Fallon bill, described by Mr. White, and the passage of Public Law 627 (condensed in the second article below), Congress was bombarded from all sides by voters and lobbyists alike, and the bill's stormy path to final enactment reflected the variety and force of the public's demand. Within a fortnight of President Eisenhower's repeated call for a gigantic modernization of the Interstate System, in his State of the Union message to the second session of the 84th Congress, Representative George H. Fallon of Maryland introduced the second highway bill to bear his name. Save that it called for pay-as-you-go financing as opposed to a bond issue, the bill contained no money-raising provision, and this feature—left to the Congress—sparked much of the ensuing debate.

As in the preceding year, congressmen who upheld the views of the trucking industry called for measures that would tax all vehicles at the same rate, with the size of the vehicle determining its total payment. Others, supporting the position of the rail-roads and of organized motorists, felt that the size of the vehicle should itself determine the rate. The ultimate compromise called for equal increases in Diesel (truck) fuel and gasoline taxes, and increased taxes equally on all sizes of tires, but it raised appreciably the levy on new trucks and buses and placed a new highway use tax on vehicles weighing over 26,000 pounds. Similar compromises—between the two houses of Congress and between the many expressions of public opinion—marked almost every provision of the bill. The House, for example, wanted to allot funds for highway construction on the basis of what each state needed to bring its part of the Interstate System up to the newly set Federal standards; the Senate wanted to follow the old method of allocating funds to each state by a formula based on population, rural mail route mileage, and geographical area. The bill signed by the President in June 1956 incorporated the Senate plan for the first three years but called for subsequent changes based on further study. Other differences—such as those over the earmarking of highway funds for highway use; repayments to the state for suitable sections of the Interstate System already completed; creation of a Highway Trust Fund to hold and govern monies raised by the act—were resolved in the same spirit, and with such success that the completed bill passed the Senate by an 89-1 margin (the lone dissenter was Senator Russell B. Long of Louisiana, who objected to the new taxes) and by a voice vote in the House.

Public Law 627, despite its provisions for the greatest highway program in history, will doubtless have to be followed by others of similar magnitude, for it is directly concerned with less than 2 per cent of our vast system of roads. It is a milestone in the nation's journey toward an adequate highway system, not the goal, for the leavening of our economy foreseen by Charles B. Seib in the concluding article will engender fresh needs as well as fresh opportunities. And the achievement of that ultimate goal —hastened with the skills described in "Highway Engineering" by George Koether; hindered by the legal and esthetic considerations raised by Philip B. Yeager and Robert Moses in "New Laws for New Roads" and "A Word of Warning"—will transform the face and future of twentieth century America as radically as the building of the railroads altered our lives and fortunes in the nineteenth.

THE BATTLE FOR HIGHWAYS—IN CONGRESS [1]

Every perspective of our country and times leads us to believe that we are only at the beginning of the automobile age, the era of complete mobility. Today, we have an automobile industry that turns out 8 million new vehicles a year. This industry has already equipped our highways with 61 million cars and trucks; in ten years there will be some 81 million in use, and in another decade the total will be almost 100 million.

What makes these figures ache is their relationship to our roads. At the outbreak of the second World War, we had about 3.3 million miles of road in this country; since then we have added about 1 per cent in new road mileage. The present length of our roads is almost permanently frozen. As we add new

[1] From "Where Are Those New Roads?" by Theodore H. White, author, foreign correspondent, and journalist. Collier's. 137:44-51. January 6, 1956. Copyright 1955 by The Crowell-Collier Publishing Company. Reprinted by permission.

automobiles, the existing lanes must, therefore, be broadened continuously. Since the war, we have worked energetically but sporadically on bits of superhighway; but in the same period the number of vehicle-miles driven in this country has doubled, and even with the new roads our traffic lanes are totally inadequate. If, at present, every registered automobile in the country took the road at the same time, we would have one car spotted every seven hundred feet on every street, every country road, every lane of every highway. And in twenty years their numbers may nearly double. Now, to any American who has let his throttle out as he turned off the cloverleaf onto one of our great new superhighways, denunciation of these great lanes must seem like nonsense. We Americans are people who thrill to road building and engineering; each new overpass, each great split-lane seems to have added dimension to our power and imagination as individuals.

Our newest state highways—the majestic Ohio Turnpike, the crowded New Jersey Turnpike, the imperial New York Thruway—are superb thoroughfares, the best of all time. But they are only stumps and pieces of a highway net. They are not a *system*. They are built only in and through limited areas where the engineers gamble that the toll fees of normal driving will repay in precisely calculated and collectible sums the enormous investment of private bondholders. They are not enough, and they dump the traffic they collect on the outskirts of our big cities in chaos and confusion.

The real problem of road building in America is new, and peculiar to our kind of democracy. In a country where every man is equally privileged and equally mobile, no citizen can be prevented from using the roads when and how he wants—even if everyone wants to use them at the same time. And, just as the arteries of our blood must be prepared to handle the emergencies of physical exertion or let us die, so the arteries of our public communication must be able to handle the convulsions of seasonal or weekly peaks in traffic or let anarchy prevail.

This is why our engineers figure that every highway must be designed to carry all normally predictable congestion (except for those thirty busiest hours of the year—the summer weekends and

Labor Day and Fourth of July hegiras—whose peaks cannot be handled except by astronomic expenditures.) This is why, too, our highways must be designed to handle any legitimate truck load.

Our roads today, fine as they may feel under the tread of normal weekday traffic, no longer meet these standards. Certain sections of our nation's choking road net are already killer belts— the Boston Post Road between New England and New York, the old Suicide Alley out of Baltimore to Washington which engineers call "Bloody One." . . . These are already notorious murder lanes.

As fast as we build, we create traffic jams. The New Jersey Turnpike, opened in 1952, is already carrying a traffic load not predicted until the early 1980's. Already, even with its new avenues of access, New York City's approaches are so congested that on a summer Monday morning when returning weekenders mingle with the truck peak, the traffic backs up so fast at the mouth of the Holland Tunnel that an athlete, running as fast as he can, could not keep up with the tail of the jam once it begins to clot backward.

All this is costing incalculable sums of money. It costs us, in addition to the cold valuation of $4.3 billion annually in accidents, another $5 billion in wastage of labor time, gasoline, rubber and equipment. It literally costs less to ship a crate of apples all the way from Oregon to the Hudson River than to get it across the Hudson to New York's East Side.

This road shortage may finally, if war comes, cost us our national life. For none of the great metropolitan areas possesses anywhere near adequate road facilities to evacuate swiftly the more than 70 million people our Civil Defense authorities estimate will have to flee.

The crisis has been swelling for a long time. But up to now our highways and roads have been in the domain of state and local governments, with the Federal Government appropriating a modest annual sum to subsidize them in their work. Last year [1955], finally, we arrived at a stage when it was obvious that the local resources and local programs could no longer meet what is now a national emergency. Which is why . . . Dwight

D. Eisenhower asked a group of five distinguished citizens, headed by General Lucius D. Clay, retired, to devise a program for meeting the crisis head on.

The Clay report that issued from their labors was hailed editorially almost unanimously, and in a few weeks, now renamed the President's Highway Program, was delivered to Congress for action. Whereupon nothing further happened except debate. For suddenly our lawmakers found themselves engaged, at the supreme level of national politics, with those forces and groups which have always, in every Statehouse, made highway politics synonymous with bitterest controversy. [For an account of the struggle at the state level, see "The Battle for Highways—In California," below.—Ed.]

The Clay proposals were not, of course, born simply out of the amateur ruminations of a number of civic-minded gentlemen enthusiastically exploring our needs over a period of a few weeks. They were, as a matter of fact, only the polished form of a dream that had slowly been maturing in Washington for twenty years.

For Washington, among other things, is a city of dreamers. Among the boldest of these dreamers have always been the engineers of our Bureau of Public Roads. And the dreams that emerged in finished form in the Clay report were born at the bureau in the darkness of the depression. At that time, some now unremembered congressman pushed through Congress a resolution calling on the bureau to scheme up a major road-building program to soak up depression unemployment. What the congressman wanted, however, was a geometrical grid across the nation—three multilane highways running east to west, three more running north to south, all of them darting up hill and down dale, straight as an arrow, with little or no relationship to the needs of the country.

The engineers of the Bureau of Public Roads soon pointed out how phenomenally uneconomic and expensive such a grid would be. But they suggested an alternate plan, called the National System of Interstate Highways, which would be something entirely different. Through the years, the dream system gradually won official recognition. Franklin D. Roosevelt blessed it as a measure to pick up postwar economic slack; Congress, in

1947, formally made its map tracings official as the outline of our future in public communications.

The Interstate System will be based on existing roads. In its improved form, as it lies on the planning boards of the engineers, it is still a dream—a spectacular in concrete, asphalt and steel. Forty thousand miles of multiple-lane highway, running between major cities, will stretch across the nation in a road net distinguished from any previous conception of engineers in capacity, durability, grandeur and sweep.

Men will be able to drive from New York to San Francisco, scarcely, if ever, slowing at a traffic light. Truckmen will grind on hour after hour, without shifting gear or slowing to the agony crawl of the upgrade. Passenger cars will sweep by them in other lanes without ever once having to poke their noses out into the perilous stream of opposing traffic. Hills will melt away and distances will evaporate.

Not only that. The Interstate recognizes the tragic plight of our strangling big cities. It is the first serious plan to cleave through the tangled approaches of our great metropolitan areas and clear broad avenues of entrance and exit through the choking metropolitan jungle and its sprawling suburban fringes. Where our present new highways stop at city limits, the Interstate will slice directly through the urban jungle of streets in spectacular expressways that will take people through the heart of metropolis and out to the open road on the other side. It will be a *system*.

The Clay program—the President's Highway Program—made the Interstate System the crownpiece of a simple three-point program.

First, it proposed that the Federal Government raise some $25 billion to spend on the great Interstate to finish it in ten years—this sum to represent 90 per cent of the total cost, the balance to be raised in the states. Thirteen billion of this would be spent on urban approaches alone. Where modern toll roads were up to the dream standards of the Interstate—some 2,500 miles of such roads exist, mainly in the North—the states which had built them would be reimbursed.

Second, it proposed that current routine Federal appropriations for highway aid to secondary and feeder roads of the great Interstate be continued at $600 million a year, or slightly less than their present total.

Third, it proposed a way for paying for the great new Interstate—that the Federal Government would set up a Federal Highway Corporation which would sell $20 billion worth of bonds, the bonds to be paid for out of current gasoline taxes, which would bring in ever more income as the new roads were built. The bonds, it was estimated, would take thirty years to pay off.

It was this third proposal that triggered off the fight. For the politics of American highways has always been dominated by one overwhelming truth: everyone loves roads, but no one wants to pay for them.

Once the great highway program reached Congress . . . all the complications of this truth began to unfold. The 1955 Battle of the Highways, as fought in Congress, proceeded in three main stages, each illuminating a separate area of uncompromising conflict.

Both of the first two stages of battle unrolled in the Senate—and . . . the first of the two Senate struggles raged over the bond-financing provisions of the Administration's highway bill.

For twenty years, the Senate had listened to Republicans denouncing Democrats as borrowers and spenders, recklessly saddling the nation with debt and burden down through all the unborn generations of time. And the Democrats had always replied that this was a healthy, growing country whose children could well afford to pay for the benefits we, their fathers, were so wisely preparing for them.

Now the sides switched. The Republican bond corporation proposal, said the Democrats, was trickery, fraudulent evasion of the legal debt limit of the nation. The bonds would eat up $11 billion of interest in addition to their principal; only bankers would profit.

It was as if, they implied, the huge $280 billion official national debt were about to spin off a satellite "corporate" debt into space, perhaps followed by others, until we had a whole constellation of satellite debts whirling about the economy, all exerting an irresistible inflationary pull. . . .

To all of which arguments, the Republicans replied as if the mantle of Franklin D. Roosevelt and all the ghosts of the New Deal had descended on them. Nothing great or creative is ever done, they said, unless one reasonably finances the present out of the future. This is what a homeowner does when he raises a mortgage on a new home, what a corporation does when it issues debentures for a new plant, what the nation must do to finance expansion in time of need.

They argued that if money were available immediately, through the bonds, to build the system now, highway use would increase so rapidly that gasoline taxes would rise enough to pay off the entire debt burden within thirty years without a single extra tax. Roads would be built, said the Republicans—and it would be painless. . . .

The Senate gravely listened to both sides, then by a resounding two-to-one vote rejected the President's bond plan. It then turned to phase two of the fight—the argument over the alternative plan . . . brought in by Senator [Albert] Gore [of Tennessee] for the Democrats. The Gore bill was quite different from the President's original proposal. It carefully omitted any financing provision at all, thus dodging that fight; the money for the highways it proposed would be found, said its proponents, by the House—where, constitutionally, all bills taxing American citizens must arise.

Deep and basic to the thinking of the Gore bill were several convictions—that the secondary and country roads would be shortchanged if the Clay proposals for pouring money into the Interstate went through; that the nation had too many other needs to commit itself irrevocably to so large a program at once; that control of the money it appropriated must rest with Congress, not with any centralized Federal agency.

Instead of biting off a ten-year chunk of the future, therefore, it limited its commitments to $7.7 billion over a five-year period, after which Congress could take another look at the problem. Another $4.5 billion would go to the lesser local roads that would feed the Interstate.

The Gore bill represented the best thinking of Senate Democratic leadership. And the Republicans . . . denounced this thinking as pitifully inadequate. It was a horse-and-buggy bill, they said, as they went on to open up another continuous area of American highway debate—the everlasting struggle between metropolitan and rural Americans about where and how roads should be built.

What the Republicans objected to most was the way the Gore bill shared the enormous funds for the Interstate among the individual states. The Clay proposal had advocated that $25 billion be spent by the Highway Corporation where needed —largely in the congested population centers of the North and East. But the Gore bill instead insisted that at least half the money be divided among the states by the traditional formula of highway aid.

Once again, as debate rolled on, the Senate sat in witness of a switch. The Democrats, normally as sensitive as sandpapered skin to big-city votes, voted solidly for the bill. Republicans, normally suspicious of big-city needs, voted solidly against it. But the Democrats had the votes and the Gore bill passed. It passed, to be shelved almost immediately. For while the long hearings and debates had dragged on in the Senate through March, April and May, the members of the House had begun to draw up their own plan—the so-called Fallon bill. . . .

Now the Fallon bill—named for Democratic Representative George H. Fallon of Baltimore, a long-time road enthusiast— was offered as a work of courage and forethought. Long before the Senate had finished consideration of the bills before it, House Democrats had decided that their road bill would be one of "real statesmanship"—which is to say that since roads have to be paid for, they would undertake to find the money. The Democrats of the Public Works' subcommittee drawing up the road bill conferred with Sam Rayburn, the Speaker, who praised their inclination and then, in a total breach with House tradition, told them to go ahead and write the taxes themselves.

The Fallon bill accepted the dream plan of the Interstate System, and the continuing Federal support of lesser roads as embodied in the President's program, altering them chiefly by spreading out the expenditures over thirteen years instead of ten. But it flatly rejected setting up any Federal corporation to borrow the money by bonds. Instead, it bracketed the appropriations it demanded with precise tax measures to meet them.

It insisted that the burden of paying for roads must fall most heavily on those who profit most by them. It called for raising the tax on every gallon of gasoline burned in our automobiles by an additional cent (at a cost to the average motorist of about $5.56 a year). Not only that. The architects of the Fallon bill were convinced that the ponderous, pounding heavy rigs of the trucking industry are the villains that beat our roads to bits [See the four articles on trucks in Section II, above.] Consequently, they proposed that heavy trucks should pay a sort of supertax—a fifty-cents-a-pound tax on every truck tire over 8.5 by 18, a special four-cent tax on each gallon of fuel for the extremely heavy Diesel trucks, a new and heavier excise tax on a new truck when purchased. Such taxes meant that the normal five-axle heavy rig would be hit by what the truckmen claimed would be an additional tax bill of some $1,031 in the first year. . . .

Two giant camps soon developed in the struggle over the bill. One was led by the railways, supported by the American Automobile Association and backed by most of the state highway officials of the country. They supported the Fallon bill. In the other were the truckmen, the tire dealers, the independent oil dealers, the Diesel manufacturers—led in the grand strategy of opposition by the truckmen.

It is easiest to begin the story of the fight over the Fallon bill with the story of the railway men. Now, the railways have an acute and continuing interest in highways. In modern America, truckmen and railway men have been as bitter and unforgiving enemies as sheepmen and cattlemen on the open range of Wyoming, eighty years ago. In the past thirty years the trucking industry has grown to be a giant that grosses over $5 billion a year for freight haulage (against the railways' $8 billion). . . .

[With] the great Interstate System, . . . with its near-level grades, its limited accesses, its numerous and heavy-paved lanes, the truckers—now engaged principally in short-run transport—will have a chance to gnaw away as successfully at the railways'

long-haul freight business as the airlines have at the railways'
long-haul passenger business, and the commuters' automobiles at
their suburban passenger business.

Any kind of legislation on the Interstate System thus placed
the railways in a delicate position. They could not, in a nation
that loves highways, simply come out and flatly denounce better
roads. Yet they could scarcely watch with blithe unconcern as
the nation proposed to build this spectacular roadbed for their
competitive rivals. They had to present their views skillfully—
by supporting the highways the nation wanted, yet making sure
their competitive rivals, the truckers, gained no advantage out of
them. Which, in essence, is why the railways threw all the influence they could behind the Fallon bill.

Robert S. Henry, who is a vice-president of the Association
of American Railroads in Washington, . . . explained the railways' position . . . thus:

Highways? Why, of course we're in favor of good highways. But
we want a *sound* highway program and any sound highway program has
to include user charges—people who benefit from it should pay, and that's
particularly true of people who use these facilities to carry on commercial
business. We railways pay in taxes 11.9 cents of every dollar we take in;
we pay 19.7 cents more of every dollar to maintain our roadbeds and
tracks. The truckers pay only 7 cents of their dollar for taxes and they
get their roadbeds free. That makes 31 cents out of our dollar against
their 7 cents. That's just not fair—and that's why we think the Fallon
bill is such a good bill.

Exactly how much influence the railways brought to bear in
the drafting of the tax features of the Fallon bill no one knows.
The American Trucking Associations, of course, holds the railways directly responsible for the taxing of big trucks. According
to John Lawrence, ATA managing director:

They have intervened in the highway program, attempting to promote punitive taxes on big trucks which will cripple truck competition
with their own freight operations. . . . Congressmen have evidence of
that on their desks in the form of a barrage of letters, wires and calls
inspired by railroad interests, and often indeed sent to their offices in
railroad envelopes. No such railroad lobby has descended on Washington
in the history of the Republic as that which is now operating in support
of the soak-the-truck proposals. It is this wrecking crew which is mainly
responsible for throwing the highway situation out of perspective.

This bitter statement must be balanced by other facts, for the truckmen, when they finally mobilized, easily matched the railway men in power and skill of influence. Their open bitterness reflects, mostly, the fact that the railways were informed of the tax measures on trucks weeks before the truckmen realized what was happening in committee. And by the time the truckmen had become aware of what was happening they found themselves trapped as if by political jujitsu.

The railways had already taken up the position of virtue; they were supporting the Fallon bill, the boldest highway program ever proposed. But the truckmen were faced with Hobson's choice. They could accept the Fallon bill, giving them the great Interstate System they so desperately wanted—yet if they did so they would have to accept a tax burden on their industry which they claimed added another $375 million a year. Or they could elect to torpedo the Fallon bill and accept the blame for sabotaging the highway program.

The truckmen elected to mobilize against the bill. And their emergency mobilization dramatically outweighed anything the railways had previously been able to muster.

Says Walter Belson of the American Trucking Associations:

Yes, we had considerable influence in killing the Fallon bill. But don't confuse the Fallon bill with the highway program. We're not such stupid idiots as to be opposed to a road program we need as much as anyone else. We were about the first group to support the highway program from the beginning. We supported it before both Senate and House, we agreed to accept increased taxes to pay for it—we'll pay our fair share, the same tax rate on fuel, tires and equipment everyone else pays. Don't misunderstand what this means in dollars. The same rate of tax will make the big truck pay five times as much as the average passenger car in gas tax every mile it runs, eighteen times as much in tire tax and thirteen times as much in equipment. This is not per company, but on every individual five-axle truck owned as against a passenger vehicle. And our state taxes run up to forty times as much per truck as per the average passenger car.

Desperately and doggedly . . . the truckmen and their allies fought to pull the tax teeth from the Fallon bill. The committee members compromised with the truckmen by moderating their original bill until the additional Diesel tax was lowered by 2 cents a gallon and the tax on large truck tires reduced from 50 cents a pound to 15 cents a pound. But the lawmakers could not be moved from their conviction that it was heavy trucks that profited most from the new roads, that heavy trucks required most of the extra-cost features of the roads—the wider lanes, the sturdier bridges, the pavings of twelve inches rather than the six or eight that might handle normal passenger traffic. A principle was involved, they said—a user charge was being imposed for the first time on a Federal level and special users had to pay special taxes. The truckmen could not accept this principle.

By the time Congress got around to voting on the revised version of the Fallon bill . . . an array of eloquent interests had all convened on Capitol Hill to protest its tax features.

The Diesel manufacturers implied their industry would be so hobbled that it might die, thereby jeopardizing the entire national-defense program, which requires Diesel engines.

The big oil companies and big tire companies protested, in the orthodox tradition, that they could not see why their products should be made into particular and peculiar tax-collecting agencies of governments. . . . Independent oil companies and independent tire jobbers protested at the taxes because, they said, it would manacle them in competition with the giants of the industry, whose capital structure could more easily afford to bear the amount of additional capital frozen into the inventory of every tire or oil outlet by the new taxes. Their lobbyists painted a somber picture before the Fallon committee of thousands and thousands of little businessmen squeezed out of business because they could not carry the taxes for their customers.

"I feel," said one of their spokesmen, "like I am representing a plucked chicken with two feathers left in his tail, and there is a hand reaching out for the last feathers."

Each of the trade associations joined in battle against the bill had roots in a thousand small towns and neighborhoods of America. Now these too began to be heard from in a lobbying campaign unmatched, say many congressmen, since the days of the Taft-Hartley bill. Telegrams began to snow on Congress

—an estimated 100,000 in all, 10,000 on Congressman Fallon's desk alone.

The telegrams were accompanied by letters. They came not only on stiff white paper under the letterheads of great firms or associations but in the grease-stained handwritten letters that worry congressmen much more—under letterheads of "Art's Filling Station," of "Alf's Friendly Service," of "Lone Star Sales and Service."

In the final days of the fray, the AFL Teamsters Union, perhaps the most powerful influence of all, got to work, as Dave Beck decided that his truckers should back up the truckmen who employed them. . . . Some congressmen claim they could even trace a trucker's day at the wheel by following the date lines of telegrams that would arrive. A driver might send his first wire from, say, Philadelphia at eight in the morning, his second from Harrisburg two hours later, his third from Pittsburgh that afternoon, his fourth from Toledo in the early morning.

By the time . . . that the final roll call on the Fallon bill took place, the House and its members were adrift under impulses and pressures they could not fathom. The drive against the bill was sharp; pointed and overwhelming; but the support for the bill, which should have come from the average motorist, was conspicuously absent.

Even though experts say that modern highways would save him $100 a year in car expenses, the average motorist was silent. Though Andrew Sordoni, the president of the American Automobile Association (himself a commercial truckman), told the House that his members supported the bill and would accept it, he could deliver few votes.

Some congressmen were deeply upset by the breach of tradition which had let a new committee write the taxes that had always previously been the sole prerogative of the august Ways and Means Committee. Even more important, many of them dimly sensed (and some were sharply informed) that the new bill, by increasing gasoline and tire taxes, was extending the taxing power of the Federal Government into the domain which the individual states had always considered as one of the reserved areas of their authority. Old-line state righters bridled.

And, finally, party discipline and control on both sides collapsed. The Fallon bill was a Democratic bill. Sam Rayburn, the Speaker, convinced of his authority and prestige, felt certain down to the last minute that party discipline would rouse the necessary votes; when, at last, he realized it could not, it was too late to improvise the tactics or counter-pressures to whip his errant Democrats into line.

The Republicans erred as badly. The White House, which had always wanted to pay for the roads by bond borrowing, came at the last minute to the conclusion that the Fallon pay-as-you-go measure was better than none. But by the time Sherman Adams had phoned this eleventh-hour decision to Republican Congressman De Witt Hyde of Maryland, voting had begun. By the time Hyde got the message to Republican floor leaders, a House colleague later recounted, the Republicans were voting almost solidly against the bill and it was too late to switch. By the resounding margin of 292 (mostly Republican) to 123 (mostly Democratic), the House had rejected the Fallon bill. . . .

THE BILL THAT PASSED [2]

The nation's biggest road building program [Federal-Aid Highway and Highway Revenue Acts of 1956, Public Law 627] . . . provides for a thirteen-year construction period beginning . . . July 1 [1956] to be financed more or less pay-as-you-build. New and increased user taxes on such items as gasoline and tires will bring in around $14.8 billion over a sixteen-year taxing period.

Present highway user taxes will be earmarked for road building, and levies, both old and new, are calculated to yield $38.5 billion in the sixteen-year period. . . .

[2] From "New Roads: Thirteen Year Look Ahead." *Business Week.* p29-30. June 30, 1956. Reprinted by special permission of *Business Week*, a McGraw-Hill publication. Copyright 1956 by McGraw-Hill Publishing Company. (This article is a condensation of the provisions of Public Law 627, a compromise measure passed by Congress and signed by President Eisenhower one year after the defeat of the Fallon bill, described in the preceding article.)

Backbone of the project will be completion of 41,000 miles of interstate superhighways [The name of the Interstate System is changed by the bill to the "National System of Interstate and Defense Highways."—Ed.] that will connect all major cities. Construction of other subsidiary roads will be stepped up, too, so that by 1969 the country will have a modern network of highways.

The Federal Government will pay the major share on the Interstate System—90 per cent with states contributing 10 per cent. [Alaska, for the first time, shares in funds for the primary and secondary systems.—Ed.] On other roads—primary, secondary, and urban—the basis will be 50-50. Under the old program, Congress for two decades has approved short-term highway aid that in general matched 50-50 the money put up by the states.

The Federal share on the interstate roads will run around $25 billion; another $2.5 billion of Federal money will be parceled out to states over the next three years to get construction under way on the other roads.

Federal spending on the highway program is expected to start out around $1 billion a year, then step up to a peak of around $3 billion a year during the mid-1960's. Later it will work down to around $1 billion toward the final years. This year, Federal aid is $875 million.

Apportionment of the interstate money will continue for three years on the present formula, based on such factors as area and population. Then it is designed to shift over to a needs basis. This means if the cost of completing a state's interstate mileage is, say, 10 per cent of the cost of completing the entire system, then the state gets 10 per cent of the year's money allocation. Congress can always change the rules.

Tax money for the road system will be put into a highway trust fund to be handled by the Secretary of the Treasury. The Administration won a provision for construction hold-downs so that the Government cannot obligate more money to states for any year than is currently in the trust fund. However, states can go ahead on new roads at their first expense, with reimbursement to come later.

Besides, receipts are certain to exceed expenditures for at least the first three years. Thus, the restriction can have no effect before the middle of 1959 at the earliest.

The sixteen-year tax period starts July 1 [1956], when the Federal tax on gasoline, Diesel, and special fuels will go up 1 cent a gallon to 3 cents; the manufacturers' sales tax on trucks, trailers, and buses will climb from 8 per cent to 10 per cent—the amount now paid on passenger cars; the Federal tax on tires will increase from the present 5 cents a pound to 8 cents; camel-back rubber for retreading will be taxed for the first time at 3 cents a pound, and trucks weighing 13 tons and over will have to pay a special yearly registration fee of $1.50 per 1,000 pounds. Taxes apply only to vehicles that normally use the roads, farm and other vehicles are exempt.

States that already have big chunks of free and toll roads that will be incorporated into the Interstate System have sought assurance that they will be paid for these roads. The new law gives them no such assurance. Studies will be made on the advisability of repaying states, with the final decision up to Congress later.

The Federal Government will reimburse states that normally pay for the cost of relocating utilities, on the same basis as the Federal-state matching on the project—90-10 on interstate roads, 50-50 for others.

Size and weight restrictions are set for big trucks using the new highways. States must keep limits at 18,000 pounds on single axles, 32,000 pounds on tandem axles, 73,200 pounds gross weight, and widths of 96 inches or at the state limits that are in effect on July 1—whichever is greater.

Construction on the interstate roads will be subject to the Davis-Bacon Act calling for Federal minimum wages.

States can get going immediately on the new road system. First actual construction is expected on some 11,000 miles of interstate roads that have already been mapped out, mainly rural mileage.

THE BATTLE FOR HIGHWAYS—IN CALIFORNIA [3]

Since the turn of the century, California had had a history of almost perpetual crisis over the highways. The state, which is more than one thousand miles long, grew up after the era of railroad building. One third of its towns have no railroad facilities. Trucks carried 85 per cent of the farm products to the Los Angeles market and 50 per cent of the state's heavy tonnage. During World War II, it was found that 65 per cent of all *passenger car* traffic had to be classified as essential.

In 1938, California's future depended upon a highway system that was falling apart at the seams. The state had been paying less and less for more and more, as the expenditure for highways dropped from 2.4 cents per vehicle mile in 1921 to less than 1 cent. The 3 cent gasoline tax had been put into effect in 1927, when there were seven thousand miles of state highway. Since then, the state highway system had doubled—but a half cent of the tax revenue had been spread to include improving city streets and connecting state highways through towns, while 1 cent had always gone to the state's fifty-eight counties. This left only 1.5 cents for a fourteen-thousand-mile system being pounded to pieces by 931,592 more vehicles traveling 8.785 billion more miles than in 1927.

During the war, the rickety highway structure really went to pieces. In 1944, the State Division of Highways listed *critical* deficiencies that would cost $629 million to patch up. California wasn't even keeping up repairs. . . .

One trouble was the lack of budgetary control; log-rolling could cause funds to be shifted from one project to another. On the county level, California had 285 independent road departments operating under a hodge-podge system almost one hundred years old. A county supervisor was permitted by law to rule his own little highway empire. The cities were in such a snarl they didn't even know their own deficiencies.

[3] From "How California Got Fine Roads" by Samuel W. Taylor, California journalist and magazine writer. *Freedom of the American Road*. Ford Motor Company. 3000 Schaefer Road. Dearborn, Michigan. 1956. p 10-14. Reprinted by permission.

By a curious twist . . . [Senator Randolph Collier of Siskiyou County] cracked this situation wide open as the opponent of a highway bill whose sponsorship he proposed to investigate. On June 16, 1945, upon his resolution, the legislature created a Joint Fact-Finding Committee on Highways, Streets, and Bridges, with the senator from Siskiyou as chairman and $100,000 for the job. . . .

The Collier Committee determined to find out what California needed for ten years ahead. This long-range view became the rallying point of the opposition in what grew into the biggest political battle in the state's modern history. But when the fight came, the committee had the facts to win public support. By putting engineering and economics ahead of name-calling and sensation, it created the pattern for a highway study which since has been duplicated in more than half of the states.

After appointing a twenty-nine-man advisory council of VIP's representing civic, farm, industrial, transportation, labor, and traffic associations, the committee hired and borrowed all sorts of experts . . . to develop the facts about California's road needs. "Then the show hit the road," Collier says. "We went to the people." There was no other place to go; the facts never before had been collected.

As the Collier Committee toured the state for a year and a half, holding sixty-four hearings in the cities and the cow counties, it not only gathered facts but presented facts to the public. It also stirred up a series of disputes.

Two of the most controversial points were Collier's idea that commercial vehicles should pay about 15 per cent of the highway bill, figured on the higher cost of building roads for heavy trucks; and his flat endorsement of a 3 cent raise in the fuel tax.

Everywhere it went, the committee found critical highway deficiencies—and people who were ready to throw their support into the job of correcting them. When the legislature met in January 1947, called in extraordinary session by Governor Earl Warren for enactment of highway legislation, the session promised to be hectic. It was.

The report of the Collier Committee, based upon the scientific findings of its teams of experts, was an impressive document. It consisted of 532 pages of dynamite that exploded as early as page 5 with the statement that the bare minimum required for the ten-year program was $2.4 billion—just twice as much as the state had spent on roads from 1912 to 1945.

The report was divided into three sections, each of which had been prepared by top-level talent. . . . From their research came four conclusions:

(1) The highway system was critically inadequate and needed immediate improvement.

(2) Along with a tax hike, the system of taxation should be revamped to distribute more fairly the load that had been heaped on the motor vehicle. The report recommended that 2,500 miles of strictly local roads be turned back to the counties, while motor vehicle taxes would pay only for the state highway system, together with a state-approved network of primary county roads and major city streets embraced in a "Master Plan." A ton-mile tax was proposed on trucks.

(3) Fundamental revisions were required in government authority. The report recommended withholding state funds for counties and cities until requirements were met. On the state level, it was imperative to cut through the fog of overlapping lines of authority and to separate highway business from unrelated duties. The report recommended that all highway policy be the function of the highway commission, and that the highway administrative budget be included in the state budget bill.

(4) Poor regulation of highway use, the report said, saw the state's roads being pounded to pieces, and more fatal accidents than New York and Pennsylvania combined. It proposed legal authority to control the weight of vehicles, and "well-tested methods of law enforcement" to reduce accidents. . . .

The basic program was established in Senate Bill 5, known as the Collier Bill. On its fate the entire plan would succeed or fail. And the reaction to SB 5 was explosive.

Powerful lobbies sprang into action, on both sides. There was opposition to tax increases in general and to the ton-mile and fuel taxes in particular. A minority of the Collier Committee scoffed at the attempt to estimate costs a decade in advance; it figured costs would go down and so no tax increase would be needed. Though, looking back, this constitutes one of the worst prophecies of the century, it should be remembered that these were honest attempts to gain the desired end by the best means available.

Despite all the pressure, the Senate remained aloof and, imbued with faith that this was what the people really wanted, passed SB 5 by a vote of 32 to 5. But this hardly worried opposing lobbyists at all. Their strength was in the Assembly, whose Committee on Revenue and Taxation completely gutted SB 5. Even Collier had to concede the bill seemed "a dead cat."

At this point, however, a public groundswell of indignation began to build up. In California, if the legislature refuses to give the people what they want, the people can initiate their own laws. Two initiative acts were being drafted; it was now quite apparent that while people didn't like taxes they demanded that something be done about highways.

To break the deadlock, a "committee of ten," five senators and five assemblymen, drafted a compromise bill, which was introduced into the Assembly by Michael J. Burns of Humboldt County, and became the historic document known as the Collier-Burns Act.

This act provided funds, mainly through a 1.5 cent increase in fuel taxes, for a ten-year program. It included modernizing the fourteen-thousand-mile state highway system, with freeways and expressways where required. The state system would include county primary systems, and state highways within city limits as well as between towns. County and city road administrations were reorganized, with controls over expenditures. The bill cleared some of the fog in state administration, and provided budget controls. And it concluded with the reminder that it furthered the policy of the state constitution, which requires highway taxes to be used strictly for highway purposes.

This compromise, which most people felt was as much as could be hoped for, sailed through the Senate by a vote of 33 to 1. On the last day of the extraordinary session—after some now-famed last-minute horse trading—it finally mustered just enough votes to clear the Assembly. Once its passage was assured, a dozen legislators climbed aboard the bandwagon, and the final vote was 53-24.

This 1947 legislation set the pattern that has become a model for other states. It not only got the highways built, but regulated the traffic upon them for efficiency and safety. The Department of Motor Vehicles was reorganized, the Highway Patrol divorced from it and given independent departmental status. Then the traffic courts were revamped (which required a constitutional amendment). From 768 courts of eight different types, the lower courts were reduced to 400 of only two types. The necessity for a judge to levy fines to hold his job was abolished, higher qualifications for judges were required, better facilities were provided, and efficiency was increased through uniform procedure.

The 1947 legislation also established the Institute of Transportation and Traffic Engineering at the University of California, which trains highway and traffic engineers, gives courses to public officials, and does research on everything from road surfaces to driver behavior.

In 1949, Collier hit the road again, chairman of a committee investigating how the 1947 law was working. Two years later his committee presented a deficiency report calling for a grand total of $3 billion in state highway spending for the next ten years—which was $1.6 billion more than current taxes would produce. This was not the shock the 1947 report had been—in fact, the public seemed strangely apathetic. An attempt was made to raise money by a bond issue, secured by future gasoline taxes, but it was turned down flat.

Once more, the committee set about the job of awakening people to their needs. And once more it called on outside experts to help with a study.

This 1952 report . . . was as readable as it was authentic. With an attractive cover, it was printed on slick paper, was well illustrated, and had five large fold-out maps. For popular distribution, it was digested to a booklet of sixteen pages, with highway problems presented not by rows of figures but by graphic layouts that drove home facts at a glance.

The selling job was no doubt a big factor in obtaining another 1.5 cent raise in the gas tax in 1953. . . . The public simply was convinced that the choice lay between good and bad roads. . . .

While figures change too rapidly in California (and in America) to have anything but comparative meaning, an idea of what goes on can be seen in these statistics: Since July 1, 1953, when the lid was finally taken off construction by the additional 1.5 cent gas tax, the state completed 209.1 miles of multiple-lane, divided expressway in the seventeen months to December 1, 1954. Completed freeway mileage rose from 90.8 to 168 miles, with 124 more miles in the works and 90 budgeted. The 1954-55 budget was $205 million—highest of any state in the nation—and yet . . . California depended entirely upon revenue from highway user taxes. When projected ten years or more ahead, relatively small increases could produce adequate funds because of the rapid rise in automobile travel mileage as the roads were built.

Since 1947, the state has doubled gasoline taxes from 3 cents to 6 cents per gallon, raised the auto license fee from $3 to $8, and added a dollar to the four-year operator's license fee. Commercial vehicles are now taxed a maximum of $67 more than the old rate for registration, and Diesel fuel taxes have risen from 3 cents to 7 cents per gallon.

The average motorist—a person who burns seven hundred gallons of gas a year—now pays an added $26.25 a year, $2.19 a month, or only 7 cents a day, for the finest highway system in the nation. . . .

If anything has been learned, it's that it is almost impossible to overestimate modern highway needs. From June 30, 1947, to June 30, 1954, exactly 2,187,143 additional vehicles took to the state's highways, for a grand total of 5,716,341. Yesterday's wildest dreams now seem quaintly reactionary. Opposition to "gold-plated highways" these days is almost exclusively confined to *future* projects. After completion, the common criticism of a highway that seemed fantastically expensive is, "Why didn't they make it big enough in the first place?" Chances are the reasons can be found in the same places, and cured in the same ways, as Collier discovered in his seventeen-year campaign.

NEW LAWS FOR NEW ROADS [4]

The nation needs one more essential element if it is to carry out what is called the most ambitious highway undertaking since the Roman censor Claudius began building the Appian Way in 312 B.C.

We have the knowledge, the materials, the plan and the desire.

Since . . . President Eisenhower signed the near-$28 billion highway bill [of 1956], we have had the money—or the means to get it.

But one big hurdle remains.

We have to improve the inconsistent, confusing, and often archaic, or nonexistent highway laws under which the road planners are laboring.

Unless these are corrected trouble is certain in developing the hoped-for high-grade national highway network.

Let's look at a few examples:

One of the most strategic of all United States highways is that which runs west from Philadelphia, through industrial Pennsylvania and Ohio to Indianapolis, St. Louis and on to the West. If a new expressway along this route suddenly encounters a stubborn Illinois farmer who declines to negotiate for a right-of-way across his farm, completion might hang fire for as much as four or five years because Illinois does not permit immediate possession of land condemned by the state; it must be first adjudicated and proper compensation paid. Moreover, Illinois makes no allowance for precedence in court proceedings for such cases. And the Prairie State is far from unique in adhering to this kind of law.

Assume an expressway is due for development between Atlanta, Georgia, and Miami. Florida has authority to condemn or buy land for future use. Georgia has no such specific authority. So Florida acquires the needed right-of-way up to the state line, but Georgia, uncertain of its power, does not. By the time

[4] From "Your State May Block New Roads," by Philip B. Yeager, lawyer, columnist for the Washington *Star,* and former editor of *Congressional Digest. Nation's Business.* 44:96-7+. September 1956. Copyright 1956 by *Nation's Business.*

the expressway is ready for construction, land values along the projected right-of-way in Georgia might rise to such a point that the state cannot afford to go ahead with the project or can do so only at greatly increased cost. This, too, is a common situation.

Assume that an east-west expressway crossing Texas is scheduled to run through Fort Worth or Dallas. Access is planned only within a mile of the city limits. Merchants protest that this will substantially cut their business. So an argument ensues over who has highway jurisdiction in this instance, the state or the locality; and since Texas law on the matter is not clearly defined, the project is indefinitely delayed.

Assume that another highway project to run from Cleveland, Ohio, to Wilmington, Delaware, reaches the Ohio-Pennsylvania line. Pennsylvania is limited by its highway code in regard to the width of the right-of-way it can acquire. Federal aid specifications for this area require a minimum of 250 feet, but state law permits a maximum of only 200 feet for the type of highway planned. The program must wait for the state to bring its law into line.

Assume a situation where Colorado, in collaboration with the Federal Government, plans to construct connecting routes from relatively isolated areas to an existing Boulder-Denver toll road. Uncle Sam's share of the money is available, but Colorado has a legal debt ceiling. If this ceiling already has been reached, special legislation may be needed.

These are but a few of the instances in which existing legal deficiencies or omission may cause trouble. Others can be found in such fields as road system classification, contracts, roadside regulation, parking authority, construction and maintenance, drainage, budgeting and accounting, traffic engineering, highway establishment and abandonment, location and design, landscaping, public utility reimbursement, and so on.

Many people, of course, have been aware of these legal stumbling blocks for years. Special studies and programs designed to alleviate them have been under way for some time by the various state highway departments, legislative advisory groups, the United States Bureau of Public Roads and a number of private research organizations. . . .

To begin with, deficiencies in existing laws must be correlated with individual engineering and financial needs to give lawmakers in the forty-eight state capitols a relatively complete picture of their highway problems.

This leads to what, in the eyes of highway experts who are trying to get a national perspective, is even more crucial: a new nonprovincial way of thinking about roads.

In other words, as lawyer, legislator and judge go about the business of modifying or building highway codes, it will be essential that the highly mobile character of present and future America be kept in mind. The country's highways must now serve one national community as well as its subdivisions.

At present there are more than 35,000 highway agencies in the United States—Federal, state, county, city and town. Most of these function independently and are responsive to different authority by law.

Obviously, this means that the problem of intergovernmental relations is one of the most severe that the new highway program faces. . . .

It is not solely a matter of Federal-state cooperation, but of interstate and intrastate coordination as well. Local road authorities must recognize themselves as component parts of state and national systems—and vice versa—and respond to these needs as well as their own.

In many cases this will require considerable revision of the law. For example, in some jurisdictions the state highway agencies, under existing codes, have no authority to consult with local road agencies on common problems or to lend so much as a single truck. County systems may be operated and maintained without consultation or contact with those running the state systems. There may be no legal requirement whatever that urban routing of through traffic be determined in the light of state or Federal needs.

In some cases state highway laws are in such a hodgepodge that roads become functionally obsolete through sheer uncertainty of what the codes permit. Michigan, which has recently been overhauling its law, had developed a highway code consisting of more than one hundred separate statutes and one thousand sections, some of them nearly seventy years old. Many states are still in that plight.

Most of the basic legal problems facing the big highway building program can be classified in one of three ways. They are primarily problems of:

1. Property and individual rights
2. Authority and jurisdiction
3. Financing

Actually, these three continuously overlap. Difficulties arising in one field usually extend into the others. But the following are the major trouble spots.

Acquisition of Land

Many problems exist here.

Perhaps the most important arises from the fact that only about a third of the states have specific authority to acquire land for future use. All states, as sovereign powers, can condemn land for public purpose upon proper compensation, but this power is normally exercised when the need is immediate. Without statutory or judicial authorization the purchase or condemnation of land for future highway rights of way may prove troublesome. This can lead to delay as well as marked increase in highway construction costs.

Another difficulty lies in the fact that some jurisdictions are authorized only to acquire easements [the right to use] across property, rather than complete title to the land. This means that, if the highway department changes its plans, the cost of acquisition is lost.

Some states can buy land for future use, but cannot condemn it for that. Some can buy only unimproved land, but not land in developed areas. Some must begin actual construction on acquired land within a given period or relinquish the property. Some have no authority to dispose of unwanted land in case a shift in population or land use requires abandoning original plans. Some highway agencies, although they may have authority to acquire land for future use, are allocated money only for construction purposes or the acquisition of land for present needs.

In still other instances, cities and townships may have authority to acquire land for future use while the state does not.

In many jurisdictions the procedure of acquiring needed rights of way is, by today's standards, obsolete. Condemnation proceedings are often slow, cumbersome and must await a jury trial and an award before the highway authority can take possession.

Immediate possession, most highway experts think, is essential if the new highway program is to proceed at anything like the pace forecast. They point to the New York law as an example of what is likely to be needed. There the state makes a survey, files plats [maps of proposed routes] with the counties concerned, together with proper notice of intent to condemn. At this point, roughly speaking, title vests in the state and the details are worked out later.

It is true that the new Federal aid bill permits the Federal Government to take immediate possession if the state requests help. But most lawyers feel that the better practice is to keep eminent domain proceedings on the state level, both from a governmental and economy viewpoint.

Control of Access

Probably no part of the highway picture creates more controversy than limiting access to modern expressways. Yet this matter reaches into the heart of the new highway program, particularly in regard to the 41,000 mile Interstate System.

Much of the Interstate System is designed to handle the high-speed through traffic, which means that new expressways must have carefully controlled access to become a part of it. That is, entrances and exits will be few and designed to avoid cross-highway traffic.

But controlling highway access is not simple.

Aside from objection by commercial interests which may look on limited access with disfavor, many highway laws are inadequate to assure controlled access.

Some jurisdictions have no authority to control access in all necessary cases. They may have it for new routes, but not existing ones.

In still other states, municipalities have no legal way to require the highway commission to consider their interests in scheduling new controlled-access highways. Yet this is highly important from many standpoints because an expressway may make profound changes in the economic and social life of cities and villages it approaches. Conversely, some highway authorities have no definite way to establish and maintain the frontage roads which may be mandatory in cases where adjacent land has been highly developed.

The trickiest problem in this area, however, involves the property rights of those whose land abuts the controlled-access highway. It is a well established legal principle that these property owners are entitled to thoroughfare access, air, light and view. These cannot be taken away without just compensation. The state, on the other hand, has the duty of providing a good highway system in the public interest and, of course, has powers of eminent domain.

At least three legal tangles result from this situation.

One is the question of whether the state, as part of its eminent domain power, has authority to acquire rights of access as well as land. The law in most states is silent on this.

The second question is how to determine when an abutting property owner has been deprived of his access rights. If, for example, the owner must travel an additional mile to get on the expressway, he has probably not been deprived of his access rights in such a manner as to warrant compensation. If he must travel fifteen miles farther to get on the highway, he may have been legally deprived of them. In this matter, the law generally remains to be made.

The third question relates to the amount and kind of damages for which highway authorities may be liable when abutting property owners sue. In cases where an acquired right of way severs a single piece of property, damage may be so great as to make it advisable to buy the whole property—if the state has that authority. What seems certain is that, as new expressways approach urban areas where land values are high, more suits will be brought. This is something state legislators may want to think about in writing new highway law.

Other access problems also exist. Expressway laws in some states, for example make no provision for more than a single type or design of superhighway where several may be needed as a guide to highway administrators. In some jurisdictions the highway commissions have authority to condemn and acquire private land, but not public land; this may mean interagency squabbles and perhaps a more devious and costly routing of new roads. Finally, where necessary land or access may be held up by litigation, there is usually no way to speed up trial; in fact, only seven states provide for this sort of thing. . . .

Debt Limits and Finance

One of the financial problems which may arise as new Federal money becomes available is debt limitation. Such restrictions exist occasionally at the state level by constitution or statute and not infrequently at the county and city level where available funds may be limited by the assessed valuations. These may need alteration to adjust to over-all highway planning.

In addition some expressway laws do not authorize turnpike authorities to pledge the credit of the state, a factor which might slow down certain jurisdictions in regard to raising their share of superhighway construction money. . . .

The Federal Aid Highway Act of 1956, which is the basis for the new long-range road-building program, is a complicated document of fifteen thousand words. Before the program gets actively under way many states will no doubt discover provisions in their own laws which conflict with the Federal act in some degree. These may need to be reconciled.

The toll-road situation provides an example. The Federal Government's long-time policy is to encourage free highways, and Federal aid legislation usually has been written to insure them as much as possible. The new law is no different. With a few exceptions it frowns on the toll-road principle. On the other hand, in recent years tolls have been finding increasing favor with the states.

Whether Congress should reimburse states for existing toll roads on the Interstate System is a question that has been deferred for several years pending a Commerce Department study. So has the determination of maximum weight-and-dimension of vehicles using Federal-aid highways. Here, too, the states may need to adjust their laws.

Frequently when new expressways are laid out or existing ones remodeled, an expensive by-product is the relocation of public utility equipment such as gas mains, power lines, drainage channels and the like.

A bothersome and persistent question is how much of this cost—if any—the state or local government should pay. The new Federal-aid act requires the United States Government to follow state law in regard to reimbursing public utilities for these costs, but in many jurisdictions the law is either obscure or inadequate for a major construction program.

Roadside Facilities

An important question of authority comes up here. Increasing conflicts are expected in areas where expressways go through concentrated urban or suburban districts. Often no overriding legal doctrine determines who has authortiy over parking and roadside facilities—or where one authority ends and another begins. Even where such doctrine or law has emerged, changes may now be necessary in light of the anticipated highway boom.

Although these are the big legal tasks that are likely to dog the new highway program, they are by no means all of them.

For instance, laws on highway accounting practices may need revision. Maintenance requirements may need to be standardized. Liability for drainage damage and unnatural run-off of water will need consideration.

Bridge specifications may require liberalization.

In short, a complete overhaul of highway codes appears essential in many cases.

If this sounds like a lot of work, it is.

Highway technology plus present concepts of good road management and effective intergovernmental relationships have far outrun the law in many areas.

This is not to suggest, however, that the problems are insurmountable within the time limits set for the new highway program.

Just how they will be overcome will have to be determined town-to-town, county-to-county, state-to-state, each in collaboration with the other up and down the line.

Highway needs are often highly individualistic, and what suffices in one place is ill-conceived for another. But it seems equally true that the day of road building on a cell basis—each unit working in isolation from the rest—has passed. The need is for integrated planning.

While the details of such planning cannot be predicted, all highway lawyers seem agreed that solutions to these legal obstacles should be worked out in the legislatures first, and only secondarily in the courts. Much more can be accomplished more rapidly by statute than by the development of case law. It is more democratic, more accurate and more certain.

Courts reverse themselves as personnel changes. But the language of a statute or highway code remains constant. In any event, it can always be amended as need dictates.

HIGHWAY ENGINEERING [5]

A modern four-lane highway can cost four, eight, sometimes ten times as much per mile to build as the two-lane roads of the twenties; it requires 420 per cent more pavement, 400 per cent more earth excavation, 1,000 per cent more steel and 7,626 cubic yards of sub-base previously not built. The old roads had two 9-foot lanes; the new ones have four 12-foot lanes. The pavement was 6 inches thick; now it is 9 or 10. The old roads had 6-foot shoulders; the new ones, 10-foot shoulders. Today, road builders literally change the face of the earth, tunneling through or leveling mountains, filling valleys, digging out bogs and refilling them with sound soil. All this costs money.

[5] From "Are We Buying Another Traffic Jam?" by George Koether, automotive editor of *Look*. Reprinted by permission from the September 6, 1955 issue of *Look* magazine, p65-9. Copyright by Cowles Magazines, Inc., 1955.

But tax-slappy Americans are asking: Will these new high-ways give better service than the highways of the twenties? Will America find itself behind another . . . highway deficit in 1980? The indications are that it will not.

While our roads have been wearing out, highway engineers, contractors and manufacturers of paving materials and machinery have learned how to make new highways as modern as the vehicles they carry. And these new roads will not only be safer, but will last a lot longer than the highways built in the twenties.

The average life of a concrete highway built in that decade was 28.2 years (of an asphalt highway, 13.5 years). A first-class concrete highway built today . . . will last fifty years and more. Why? A lot has been learned about soil and sand, rock and cement, water and weather in the past two decades. . . .

In 1893, a small bureau in the Department of Agriculture, called the Office of Public Roads Inquiries, was created to investigate the best methods of road making. Up to that time, America's only paved roads were made of macadam, a mixture of stones held in place by pulverized rock, watered, during construction, to serve as a cementing medium. These roads, which had served America's horses and wagons for almost a century, failed under automobile traffic. The rubber-tired motor cars sucked up the dust and the wind carried it away. Then the stones became loosened and the roads went to pieces because the wear from rubber tires failed to form new binders as had the wagon wheels and horses.

Early solutions to the automobile problem were the country plank roads, "corduroy" roads made of logs to cross swamps, and wood-brick and stone pavements in the cities. Later came asphalt and concrete. Hard-surfaced highway building had hardly got started when World War I, with its unpredictable traffic volume of heavy war matériel, gave our "new" highways their first tough test. The rapid and complete failure of many costly roads faced highway officials with a challenge. By 1920, it was apparent that traffic demand exceeded the strength of existing roads. In June of that year, the first famous road tests were begun—in Bates, Illinois, and Pittsburg, California. Of 63 test sections in the

Bates test, 22 were brick, 17 asphalt and 24 Portland cement concrete. Of the 63 sections, only 13 stood up under the pounding
of 23,200 round trips by loaded Army trucks. Ten of these sections were concrete and the other three sections, surfaced with
other materials, were built on concrete sub-bases 6 inches or more
thick. A new principle emerged from these tests: A road is no
stronger than its base.

Engineers now knew that roads had to be designed as structures, not simply as wearing surfaces to be laid like blankets over
the earth. But the highway builders of the twenties could not
foresee the oncoming weight and volume of traffic to be imposed
by World War II. In view of that unforeseen load—at a time
when labor and material priorities prevented proper maintenance
—it is no wonder our highways went to pieces. The wonder is
that they held up as well as they did.

After World War II, road tests were resumed. In June 1950
the controversial Maryland road tests were conducted. Eight
trucks lumbered for six months, day and night, rain or shine,
over a 1.1 mile test section of U S 301—a concrete road built in
1941 to handle a load limit of 20,000 pounds. The trucks varied
in weight from a single-axle load of 18,000 pounds to tandem-
axle loads of 44,800 pounds. The mileage run up was equivalent
to 19.6 years of use on one section of the road and 91 years of
use on another. Twenty-eight slabs of this test road had been
built over a granular sub-base similar to those now specified for
any good concrete highway. The remainder of the slabs were
located on a fine-grained plastic soil.

When the test was finished, all twenty-eight slabs built on
the granular sub-base were in perfect condition. In the other
sections, built on the plastic soils, "pumping" developed. That
is, water, softening the subsoil, turned it into mud. The heavy
trucks, rolling over the pavement joints, caused the slabs to bend.
This action "pumped" the mud out at the joints and edges until,
finally, the slab ends cracked because there was no underlying
material to support them.

The Maryland road test reports brought about a violent controversy between truckers and "good road" enthusiasts. Trucks
were damned as the villains of our highway breakdown. Over-

looked was the fact that government authorities had deliberately encouraged violation of their own weight limits under the exigencies of war. Overlooked, too, was the fact that all twenty-eight concrete slabs of the test road, built over a granular sub-base, came through perfectly.

But more than good pavement and a good sub-base are required for good roads. The soil beneath actually bears the traffic load. Having established the importance of the sub-base, the engineers now . . . study the soil itself. . . . In pits six feet deep, they are recreating the actual soil conditions underlying highways all over the nation, testing temperatures, humidity, resistance to impact and stress—all under laboratory-controlled conditions.

From these laboratories have come improvements in highway technique which are already paying off. . . . One improvement, beginning as an accident, was the development of air-entrained concrete. In an Eastern cement plant, lubricants from machinery got into the cement mix. It was soon discovered that concrete made with this batch of cement forestalled the "heaving" that normally occurred due to freezing of water soaked up by the pavement. Moreover, the surface of this concrete did not "scale" following applications of salt used by highway departments to melt surface ice. Research disclosed that a fatty substance, when mixed with concrete, formed billions of tiny air bubbles—100 billion per cubic yard—in the concrete slab. These bubbles, as small as .0006 of an inch in diameter, provided expansion chambers where water, turning to ice, could expand without exerting an inner stress on the slab itself. Today thirty-two states require air-entrained mixes for all new concrete highways.

Another improvement was the development of the sawed joint. In the twenties, concrete slabs were laid with wide expansion joints left open and later filled with sealing material. These sealing strips gave motorists a thump-thump-thump effect when they drove over a concrete highway. Today, the concrete is poured in a continuous ribbon, then sawed with power tools equipped with diamond blades. Construction time is speeded and the joints, much narrower, require less sealing compound. The thump-thump-thump is eliminated. The motorist gets a

quieter, smoother ride and the pavement is much less subject
to water infiltration.

One big money-saving improvement was the development of
soil cement, a simple mixture of pulverized soil with measured
amounts of Portland cement and water, compacted to high
density. This low-cost pavement can often be made from the
roadway soil at hand. Since soil constitutes 85 per cent of the
material needed, soil-cement highways are economical indeed.

Although highway building and management are under
political control, taxpayers benefit by highly competitive private
enterprise in the development of paving materials, road-building
machinery and construction methods. . . . Cement and asphalt
makers fight for every mile of road-building business. Most of
our paved roads and streets are built with asphalt. But two
thirds of our toll-turnpike mileage and three fourths of our
heavy-duty rural expressways are concrete. The competition between asphalt and cement makers has improved the quality of
both products and enabled each to serve better the particular uses
for which they are best suited.

Competition between the makers of road-building machinery,
too, is as hot as that between Chevrolet and Ford. Today the
making of earth-moving machinery is a billion-dollar business.
Since 1941, the horsepower and load capacity of earth movers
have doubled and top speeds have increased by one third. In
1924, a record for a paving crew in Pennsylvania was 464 feet
in an hour. Last year on the Ohio Turnpike, contractors aver-
aged 4,200 feet per hour. As recently as 1948, each billion
dollars of highway building required 125,000 job-site workers.
In 1954, only 78,000 workers were required for the same output.
Such savings are vital if America is to be able to afford the safer
highways it needs. Machinery makers and contractors are making them possible. Last year, the highway-building cost index
dropped back to the 1948 level. In 1927, the cost of moving
earth was 50 cents per cubic yard. Now it is 35 cents or less,
even with today's inflated dollar.

Competition among the contractors is as heated as it is among
machinery builders. There were 41,473 bids on 6,190 Federal-aid
highway projects in 1954, and last year, 1,300 contractors went

"bottoms up." On one fourteen-mile stretch of the Indiana Turnpike, the winning bid . . . was only $14,000 under the next bidder. To win another bid for a twenty-eight mile, $15-million stretch on the same turnpike . . . [the contractor] had to figure out a logistical problem worthy of a war college. He had to estimate the cost of building 39 bridges, buying 450 acres of land to obtain dirt fill, moving 6 million cubic yards of earth and 15 carloads of steel, erecting a $250,000 aggregate plant and a bulk-cement mixing plant, digging wells and connecting a special 2-mile power line, buying new Euclid scrapers costing as much as $70,000 each. He had to calculate the cost of operating 45 pieces of road-building machinery, 8 portable repair vans, 8 radio-equipped scout cars for supervisory personnel. And he had to calculate the wages of 800 men who man the scrapers, bulldozers, giant cranes and other equipment. Twenty years ago . . . twice the manpower and five years would have been required to do the job which now takes two years.

The men, machinery and know-how are ready to build America a modern road system.

A WORD OF WARNING [6]

After years of agitation, we finally have got a fairly good Federal highway law, which will gradually close the gap between car and road.

Measured by mileage, cost, and the problems it will raise, this is a huge program. It will give us a 41,000-mile network of interstate, limited-access superhighways. It will take thirteen years to complete, and will put a heavy strain on our available design and construction talent. The total Federal contribution, plus matching funds put up by the states, will come to more than $50 billion. This is the most massive public-roads undertaking of all time.

[6] From "The New Super-Highways: Blessing or Blight?" by Robert Moses, head of the New York City and New York State Park Systems and winner of the $50,000 first prize in the General Motors contest: "How to Plan and Pay for the Safe and Adequate Highways We Need." *Harper's Magazine*. 213:27-31. December 1956. Copyright 1956 by Harper & Brothers. Reprinted by permission of *Harper's Magazine*.

But before we toss our hats in the air and shout "Hosanna!" we had better take a look at the horrors as well as the advantages which the new system can inflict on us—unless we are suspicious, far-sighted, civic-minded, and unselfish, and unless we promptly tell our legislators and administrators what we want done. When Pandora let the flying pests out of her box, they say, Hope remained. Well, there is still Hope.

What are these evils? They lurk in every foot of frontage, every acre of land bordering the new routes. Even the express arteries, with limited access and infrequent entrances, will be entirely unprotected by the new Federal law against signs and billboards. The entrances, exits, and intersections are all left exposed to an indiscriminate mushroom growth of ugly filling stations, hot-dog stands, and all the other familiar roadside eyesores.

Consequently, we face the prospect of speedways built in gasoline gullies, obliterating scenery and confined between continuous rows of offensive advertising. Let's not forget that these horrors are put up by devilishly ingenious promoters whose purpose is to exploit a captive audience. They expect to cash in handsomely on great public works to which they have made no special contribution and for which we owe them nothing.

An objective so . . . against the public interest must be combated and controlled. The tendency will be to compromise, in traditional American political fashion—to find some happy definitions which will give the billboard, gas, and lunch-stand interests a break by limiting them to certain areas, distances back of the road, sizes, lighting, times of the year, etc. The trouble is that no compromise will do. This threat must be turned back at the start, or it never will be. . . .

As a justification for Federal aid, the new law requires that government officials set high standards to insure uniformity and continuity of the roads. It provides that construction standards shall be adopted by the Secretary of Commerce in cooperation with the state highway departments. The National Association of State Highway Officials has now drawn up a voluminous set of standards covering widths of roadways, divider strips, composition of pavements, curvatures, strength of bridges, and a host of other engineering and construction details.

But nowhere in these elaborate specifications is there any provision for control of billboards and advertising devices. If the billions of public investment in these new thoroughfares are to be protected, and the value of our scenery and natural assets is to be preserved, steps to prevent the onslaught of commercial advertising *must* be taken before construction gets under way.

What should be done about it? Well, first and foremost, the Federal highway law should be amended at the next session of Congress to provide minimum standards for the protection of the new highways from advertising, and to require all agreements between the Secretary of Commerce and the state highway departments to include these standards. Specifically, signs should be forbidden within five hundred feet of the property line of any right of way in the new interstate system. The amended act should authorize the states or their municipal subdivisions to supplement this basic prohibition by local regulations with even more restrictive provisions. Exceptions should be limited to necessary directional signs and official notices, signs indicating the sale or leasing of the property upon which they are located, and (in commercial areas) signs advertising a business conducted on the premises.

It will be no simple task to persuade Congress to accept such forthright amendments. The billboard industry will immediately marshal its army of lobbyists, lawyers, representatives, and stooges and launch an intensive battle to defeat them. These interests are rich and powerful, and their methods are devious. Whenever regulatory legislation is introduced, they attack on several fronts at once. They organize groups of roadside operators, on the ground that roadside control of *any* kind is a dangerous precedent. They enlist the aid of labor-union leaders, on the theory that sign painters and carpenters may be thrown out of work. They tell the farmers that they are in danger of losing billboard rentals.

One of their first maneuvers will be to minimize the horror of the billboard blight and to ridicule the people who are working to keep our roadsides clean. They will claim that their opponents are only a small group of esthetes, "garden-club gals," and misguided conservationists who object to handsome, educational, roadside frescoes. They sometimes go so far as to say that some of their work is an improvement on nature; their impudence is boundless.

With mock seriousness, their well-paid lawyers will solemnly argue that the amendment we propose would be illegal—that it would impair the constitutional rights of the billboard barons and constitute a confiscation of property without compensation. But . . . there are abundant legal precedents sustaining the validity of regulatory sign laws. The courts have repeatedly ruled that the regulation of outdoor advertising and the exclusion of commercial billboards in certain areas are in the public interest and well within the limits of the police power. Indeed, the courts have recognized that the billboard is an intrusion which distracts the traveler and endangers his safety. . . .

It has long been the cry of billboard lawyers that the courts will not recognize beauty and esthetics as factors to be considered within the limits of the police powers. Recently these lawyers got a severe jolt when the unanimous Supreme Court of the United States, in sustaining the District of Columbia Redevelopment Act of 1945, held that

> The concept of the public welfare is broad and inclusive. The values it represents are spiritual as well as physical, esthetic as well as monetary. It is within the power of the legislature to determine that the community should be beautiful as well as healthy, spacious, as well as clean, well-balanced as well as carefully patrolled.

A clever maneuver of the billboard industry is to offer cooperation in control by "voluntary agreements" with public officials in charge of highways. Many such agreements have been made. Most of them are of no value. The claim that cooperation will accomplish more than legislation is false. The record conclusively establishes that in practice self-policing is a farce.

The battle of the billboards has been in progress for several decades in our legislative halls and courts. It is a lurid chapter in the history of the highway system. Our victories represent a slow, irregular advance toward the ultimate goal of eliminating profiteering and halting the ruin of the American countryside. In the early 1920's the New York legislature enacted a law to control advertising in the Adirondack Park and thereby saved one of the state's greatest natural assets from despoilation. Shortly afterward, the legislature, after a bitter fight, enacted another law banning billboards and regulating other signs within five hundred feet of any state park or parkway. Through strict enforcement, the State Park Commissions have been able to protect the beauty of New York's parkway system and its investment of millions of dollars for landscaping, ornamental bridges, and other features which make for safe and pleasant driving.

New York City, through an amendment to its zoning resolution, also safeguards its parkways, expressways, and many boulevards and thoroughfares against this kind of intrusion. Some other cities, towns, and villages in New York have contributed to the program by local zoning laws and sign-control ordinances. In these more progressive communities, the usual rule is to prohibit all billboards and business signs in districts zoned for residence use and to prescribe the size and types of signs which may be maintained in commercial areas.

When the five-hundred-mile New York State Thruway, which connects New York City with upstate New York and New England, was first authorized in 1942, efforts were made to write into the enabling legislation a provision to control commercial advertising along the right of way. The billboard boys immediately came forward with the argument that—while it might be lawful to control signs along landscaped parkways, since they were designed for passenger vehicles only—this rule could not be extended to cover a Thruway built for use by buses and trucks as well. They argued that the commercial aspect of the new Thruway entitled them by law and equity to use it for commercial advertising. Thus they killed several bills and delayed action by the lawmakers for ten years.

In 1952, when construction of the Thruway was under way, the legislature finally passed a law authorizing the Thruway Authority to prohibit billboards and to control other types of signs within five hundred feet of the right of way. The resulting benefits are attested to by all who now travel this road. There is no reason why similar benefits should not be enjoyed by the millions who are looking forward to pleasant journeys on interstate highways authorized by the new Federal law.

Under the provisions of this law, only limited-access highways are eligible for a 90 per cent contribution by the Federal Government. No state can add any entrances to or exits from the highway in addition to those approved by the Secretary of Commerce. There is a further provision that the Federal Government will not convey back to any state the outside five feet of any right of way unless the state has provided satisfactory control of access from the abutting lands. This means that the new limited-access roads will automatically exclude all roadside business which requires direct access to the roadway. The only roadside business which does *not* require direct access to the highway on which it faces is the billboard business. All that billboards need is visibility. Why should the new law give the billboard industry this preferential treatment and free subsidy at the expense of the public?

Control of the billboard menace can best be insured by incorporating a regulatory provision in the new Federal highway law. In addition, the act should provide other remedies for use by the public officials who are charged with the responsibility of constructing up-to-date, safe, and attractive highways and keeping them free from eyesores. For example, ever since its enactment the Federal Highway Act of 1940 has provided that the construction of highways by the states with Federal aid might include "roadside and landscape development." And the 1940 act expressly authorized "the purchase of such adjacent strips of land of limited width and primary importance for the preservation of the natural beauty through which highways are constructed." Thus we find that in the 1940 law there was what amounted to a mandate from Congress to spend Federal funds to buy the strips of land needed to preserve natural scenic beauty.

Why not? Why wasn't this provision—or something like it —carried forward into the 1956 act which was the subject of lengthy debate at both the 1955 and 1956 sessions of the Congress? The public is entitled to an honest answer.

It was no inadvertent omission. The answer is to be found in the pressures of the billboard lobby. This important provision should be restored. . . . In the process it should be clarified and reduced to simpler language.

Some state highway officials, confronted with the job of protecting their roads without the backing of a sign-control law, have sought to achieve their purpose by acquiring what are known as "scenic" and "billboard" easements in the bordering privately-owned land. By this device the landowner relinquishes to the state or municipality for all time his right to erect signs of any kind within the area described in the agreement—usually a strip at least a thousand feet wide. In some instances, these easements also restrict the removal of trees and shrubs and prohibit the erection of structures which would mar the scenery.

After the original anti-billboard amendment designed to protect the new New York Thruway had been killed in the state legislature, the Superintendent of Public Works quietly acquired a number of these scenic easements along the route of the new road as insurance, in case the Thruway sign-control law might not survive the onslaughts of the billboard interests. The New York State Power Authority, which is building the enormous hydroelectric power project on the St. Lawrence River, is now acquiring similar billboard easements along the power and seaway improvements in the international section of the river.

This device has been used in other states, notably Virginia, where scenic views along the beautiful Blue Ridge Parkway have been preserved against the intrusion of roadside nuisances. Maryland and Ohio have also used the easement method to protect portions of their highway frontage from blight.

The "scenic easement" method is not, however, the final answer to the problem. While the amounts paid for these easements are usually relatively small, the procedure is cumbersome and in some locations costly. Nevertheless, authority to use the easement method as a supplement to direct statutory control should be provided in the new Federal highway law. This can be accomplished by a simple addition to the language of Section 109 of the act which provides for the acquisition of rights-of-way by the Federal authorities. There should be added to the statement of the purposes for which lands or interests in land (which includes easements) may be acquired, the words "and to preserve the natural scenic beauty of the interstate system and adjacent areas."

Let us turn now from billboards to filling stations. The provision in Section 112 of the new law forbidding the construction of gas stations on the highway rights of way should be dropped, and replaced by a provision permitting the states to construct or authorize publicly-owned and -controlled filling stations on land within the rights of way of the new limited access roads. Drivers should not be subjected to the inconvenience and danger of having to drive off the express highway, and then on again, each time they need gasoline, oil, water, air, a rest room, or food and drink.

This ridiculous prohibition against supplying on-the-highway services—which motorists have become accustomed to and now demand—will cause increased traffic congestion at the entrances and exits and will produce a motley conglomeration of gas stations, hot-dog stands, roadside vendors, honky-tonks, and glaring signs at exits and entrances, at corners of intersecting roads, and on the service roads paralleling the new expressways. We now have had sufficient experience in designing and operating controlled-access roads to know that the service needs of the travelers can best be supplied by well-designed, attractive, and publicly-controlled service stations located on the shoulders of the road or in widened center strips.

The cost of adding these convenient and attractive facilities will be infinitesimal in the large picture. Such costs can be charged directly against the project, or they can be paid off over a period of years by arranging with the operator of the station to repay the state's investment in the buildings out of gross income from his business. Both methods of financing have been used successfully on our existing parkways and expressways. In this way, proper locations can be selected and prices and quality of service can be controlled. If charges of favoritism or collusion are feared, public bidding for the service station contracts may be required; or the stations may be apportioned fairly among a number of different oil companies or their accredited filling-station operators. . . .

Local action . . . is needed to ward off the danger of ugly nests of gas stations, hot-dog stands, billboards, and other road-side eyesores at the exits and entrances and at the corners of intersecting roads. Before approving plans and turning over the large sums of construction money to the states, the Federal officials should make certain that the states and municipalities have provided adequate control of roadside development through their local zoning laws or other regulatory measures.

This is especially important in view of the fact that the construction and design standards adopted by the state highway officials will permit intersecting roads to cross the new expressways at grade in rural areas. These exposed corners will be prime targets for the enterprising builders of roadside blights. It has been said that the new highway program will help cities remove deteriorating slum areas and upgrade surroundings. We earnestly hope that it will not be said at some future date that the new highways actually created new rural and suburban slums, through failure to control roadside development.

Washington will be the control center of the new program. There all important decisions will be made, and there the huge sums of construction money will be parceled out. The new laws provided for the appointment of a Federal Highway Administrator to administer the program. The President has named Mr. Bertram D. Tallamy, now chairman of the New York State Thruway Authority, to fill this important post. Mr. Tallamy . . . is an experienced administrator and road builder fully capable of shaping our national highway policies. He will get the program off to a good start in its early critical years and, in so doing, will undoubtedly keep in mind the dictate of our Supreme Court that the concept of public welfare includes esthetic as well as monetary values.

This new highway program will affect our entire economic and social structure. The appearance of the new arteries and their adjacent areas will leave a permanent imprint on our communities and people. They will constitute the framework within which

we must live. The importance of protecting them from ruination
by uncontrolled roadside development cannot be overstated . . .
[and] remedial measures must be adopted to preserve from destruction the vast areas which will be opened up by the new
roads.

THE ROAD AHEAD [7]

The Interstate System, authorized by Congress . . . calls for a
network of highways totaling 40,000 to 42,500 miles. They will
nearly all be of high-speed, four-to-eight-lane construction, with
limited entrance and exit. The network will crisscross the nation,
linking just about every city of more than 50,000. When finished, it will constitute only 1.2 per cent of the country's total
highway mileage, but it will carry close to 25 per cent of the
total highway traffic.

Because of the complexity of planning and building a
modern highway, because the program is starting practically
from scratch, because more than half the money will be spent on
especially complicated urban projects—for these and other reasons
it is going to take many months to get the program into high
gear. . . . The general outlines of the interstate network have
been laid out, but specific routes have been selected for only
about eleven thousand miles. Federal officials believe that fewer
than ten thousand miles of the ultimate system will use present
roadbeds; the balance will be built from scratch over newly purchased rights of way. So far, rights of way have been acquired
and detailed plans drawn for only a minute part of the total
mileage.

During the next several years, residents of areas affected by
the Interstate System—which means virtually every population
center in the country—can expect to hear long, loud debate over
location of the new roads, purchase of rights of way, financing
the state and local shares of the costs, the pros and cons of
limiting access to the new highways, and so on. Also, motorists
and businessmen, particularly in the cities where the system will

[7] From "New Roads: Changed Business Pattern Ahead," by Charles B. Seib,
acting Sunday editor of the Washington *Star* and frequent contributor to magazines.
Nation's Business. 44:32-3+. July 1956. Copyright 1956 by *Nation's Business.*

bring new throughways, can expect to go through a period of detours and other construction nuisances.

While the new program is important to every citizen, it means different things to different people. Here is what it means to some major groups:

Motorists

. . . To finance the new roads, the average motorist will pay an additional $8.60 annually in Federal excise taxes, mostly the result of the one-cent-a-gallon gasoline tax increase. In addition, he may have to pay some additional state and local taxes as those governments try to pay their part of the highway bill. But, in return for these higher tax payments, the motorist will get a highway system which, say the experts, in urban areas will cut driving time and operating costs in half and be twice as safe. In rural areas it will save less time and operating costs but will be four times as safe.

The long-distance motorist will find that he can bypass or traverse at forty to fifty miles an hour cities he once crept through at an exasperating, stop-and-start ten to twenty miles an hour. He'll find himself able to travel farther and faster on his business and vacation trips. . . . For city workers and shoppers, the urban sections of the interstate system will provide quicker, safer travel between downtown commercial and business sections and sub-urban areas.

The Federal Bureau of Public Roads figures that the dollar-and-cents savings to the motorist resulting from the new system will average about one cent a mile—mostly due to the elimination of urban stop-start driving. This penny a mile means an annual saving of $94 on the 9,400 miles the average motorist drives. There will be few drivers who won't get a substantial return on their $8.60 in additional taxes if the predictions hold true.

Even more important than the saving in time and money will be the saving in lives. Figures show that the traffic toll to date is twice the total battle deaths in all our wars and that forty thousand people will be killed on the roads this year.

Secret of the safety that will be built into the . . . System is controlled access, the limiting of entrances into and exits from

from the new highways. Congress wrote controlled access firmly into the law under which the system is to be built.

Highway engineers say a chief cause of accidents—as well as the chief reason for slower movement of traffic on today's highways—is the indiscriminate entry and departure of vehicles. The combination of frequent intersecting side roads and roadside facilities make the average busy highway a succession of hazards. Traffic crossing the Interstate System will be handled on overpasses and underpasses. Cars, trucks and buses will enter and leave only at clover-leafs, ramps or other well designed interchanges except in a few sparsely settled areas. Owners or tenants of property bordering the new highways will be barred from direct access. Restaurants, gas stations, motels or other services will be barred from the right of way and will be available only on so-called service or feeder roads.

The engineers can cite impressive figures demonstrating that controlled access means more safety. They can show that existing highways with full control of access have only one third to one half as many accidents and fatalities as those with no control. The fatality rate on the controlled highway is only about 2.8 per 100 million vehicle-miles, compared with 8 per 100 million vehicle-miles on a road with no control. There is a comparable difference in the accident rate. The effect of the new highway system on the nation's driving safety record may permit a reduction in insurance premiums.

Controlled access does not mean that the new Interstate System is designed primarily for the cross-country traveler. The fact is, according to the Bureau of Public Roads, that only 2 per cent of the traffic at any given spot on the system will be transcontinental. Most drivers will be making trips of one hundred, fifty, ten miles or less. Many of them will be taking children to school, going shopping, commuting, going to visit nearby friends or relatives. Government experts emphasize that, although entrance into and departure from the interstate highways will be carefully controlled to insure optimum safety and a smooth flow of traffic, the interchanges will nonetheless be frequent and conveniently located for local motorists.

What drawbacks does the program present so far as the motorist is concerned? There will be the short-range inconvenience of intensive highway construction. This will be less noticeable in rural areas, since most of the roads in the new system will not occupy presently traveled routes. But in cities, the construction of throughways—with all the coincident razing of buildings, relocations of homes and businesses and detours—is likely to cause some temporary inconveniences.

Then there will be the higher Federal excise taxes and the chance of state and local tax increase to make up the non-Federal 10 per cent of the cost. . . .

Businessmen

Most businessmen will be affected in some way by the highway program. Some can expect to benefit from swifter and cheaper transportation of raw and finished materials. Some will even relocate their factories or warehouses near one of the new roads.

Some firms will benefit by taking part directly in the highway construction program—either by building the roads or supplying materials or roadbuilding equipment. Some businessmen will set up new gasoline stations, restaurants, motels and other services on service and feeder roads to cater to the users of the system. Others who own these types of businesses along existing routes may be hurt either temporarily or permanently by the diversion of traffic to the new highways. Many industries —auto, truck and bus manufacturers, gasoline companies, tire makers, to name a few—are expected to feel a profitable backwash from the increased travel the Interstate System will cause.

Probably the most hotly debated feature of the program so far as the business community is concerned is the bar on entry or exit other than at regular interchanges. This foreclosing of what would otherwise be attractive business opportunities, plus the expectation of damages due to relocation of routes or the conversion of existing routes to controlled access, has already caused some protests. Federal officials admit that some people will get hurt. But, they add emphatically, the damage will be much less than anticipated and will be more than outweighed in any given community or area by the spur to business the new highways will provide. . . .

Frank Turner, assistant to the Commissioner of Public Roads, maintains that studies of past projects involving the relocation of roads and controlled access on the new roads show "almost without exception that the diversion did not hurt business and in the majority of cases helped it."

He explains that in most cases the old road, with its service establishments, becomes in effect a service road for users of the throughway. Suitable connections are provided so that the motorist who wants to refuel, eat or spend the night can easily and quickly cut over to the service road and use the facilities there. This sort of arrangement is expected to be used frequently along the Interstate System.

Despite these reassurances, many businessmen are making plans now to ease the impact of the program. For example, J. Pendleton Gaines of the Florida Motor Court Association recently suggested that access roads be placed so that present business areas in rural sections would be used in most cases to meet the needs of users of the new roads, that existing highways be used as service roads when they parallel or intersect the new highways and that directional signs and printed material be used to guide motorists to the existing off-highway facilities.

One by-product of the new Interstate System is likely to be a boom in land values near the new highways. Despite controlled access, the experience of the toll throughways has been that industrial plants, residential subdivisions, shopping centers and other developments will cluster along the new roads, particularly at interchanges. Government experts figure that one third to one half of the total increase in property values as a result of the new roads would pay the cost of the Interstate System.

Figures from toll road experience support the land boom expectations. Roadside land that sold for $600 an acre before the Northern Sacramento Freeway in California was built climbed to $10,000 an acre within a few years after the freeway came. Land along the New York Thruway near Syracuse sold for about $700 an acre in 1951 and for $6,000 an acre last year.

It was estimated that even before the New York Thruway was finished, some $150 million in new plant investment along the right of way had been planned. . . .

Truckers

Trucking is expected to grow faster as the new Interstate System emerges. There are now 7 million commercial trucks on the road, and the industry expects the number at least to double by 1975.

The new highways, the trucking industry feels, will persuade more and more industries to decentralize—to expand to small towns where land and building costs are cheap, labor is available and wage levels lower.

It says business will benefit from more flexible service—quicker delivery and pick-up, loading and unloading, handling of smaller batches of goods.

Truckers will have to pay more than the private motorist toward the Federal share of the highway costs, of course. Some of the tax increases apply only to trucks—the new highway use tax on vehicles of 26,000 pounds or more for example. Also, the tax boosts on gasoline and tires hit truckers harder than motorists because of the lower mileage trucks get from each gallon of fuel or pound of rubber.

The American Trucking Associations estimate that the cost of operating a light truck will climb by more than $75 a year under the new tax schedules and the cost of operating a big five-axle job by $565. The Bureau of Public Roads estimates the average cost increase at about $185 annually per truck.

On the other hand, there have been estimates that the trucking industry will save as much as $1.5 billion a year. Faster trips will reduce labor costs (although the truckers say not by as much as many people think), less stop-and-start driving will reduce fuel consumption and tire and brake wear. Increased safety will reduce insurance costs. This, of course, is on top of the increase in business expected to result from the new highways.

The new law does put one major restriction on the truckers. It includes size and weight ceilings designed to protect the new roads from ever heavier trucks.

Truckers aren't too upset about these restrictions, however, since they do not apply in states which already have in effect more lenient ceilings, and they are at least as liberal as the restrictions now in effect in most states.

Labor

Federal officials estimate the highway program will, by 1961, provide more than 500,000 additional jobs in actual construction of the roads, in industries supplying materials and machinery, in service industries catering to the highway users and in road maintenance work.

The number of on-site highway workers is expected to increase from the present 220,000 to about 350,000 by 1958.

The road-building industry feels that finding men to fill these jobs will not be a problem.

The industry does expect trouble, however, in finding an adequate supply of engineers. In fact, an American Road Builders Association task force study indicates that the engineer shortage will be the most serious threat to fast expansion of the program.

Organizations interested in the highway program are pressuring state highway departments to beef up salary scales and other job benefits.

Efforts are being made to increase the number of highway engineering scholarships to entice more talented young men into that line of work. These organizations are also studying ways to increase the productivity of each engineer—standard plans for highway structures, aerial map-making and surveying, photographic reproduction of drawings, the use of high-speed computers to do complex mathematical work. The experts believe that by these and other streamlining techniques the total number of engineers required for each $1 billion worth of highway construction can be cut in half.

Farmers

About one out of every ten passenger cars and more than one out of every four trucks belong to farmers. Almost 90 per cent of all farm products now reach their markets via highways. These few statistics illustrate the importance to farmers of fast, safe roads.

Nonetheless, the farm groups were not unanimous in endorsing the Interstate System. The National Grange supported the program, arguing it would "free increasing amounts of state highway revenues for roads off the Interstate System." Grange National Master Herschel D. Newsom pointed out that hard-surfaced roads constitute less than a fourth of all rural roads and that 1,124,000 miles of rural roads, or some 37 per cent of the total, still have no surface at all. Calling these roads the missing links between many farms and the new superhighways, Mr. Newsom said his group would now fight for attention to these back roads. The fact that the Federal Government is stepping up its spending on the regular highway aid program should mean that the state can devote more attention to rural roads, he declared.

On the other hand, the American Farm Bureau Federation opposed the highway program all the way, taking the position that the states could do the same job better if the Federal Government would give them the exclusive right to assess gasoline taxes. The Federation took the position that the Interstate System would be of little benefit to farmers compared to the benefits of spending similar amounts of money on improving farm-to-market roads.

The States

The states will actually do the spending for the new highways. The Federal Government will put up most of the money [90 per cent], approve plans and inspect the results, but it will be the state highway departments that let the contracts and oversee the construction. In many cases this suddenly increased responsibility will call for a modernization and strengthening of state highway departments.

State officials will also have to raise the money for their share of the highway costs, recruit engineers and administrators, meet the pressures and protests from businessmen, landowners and other groups who want or don't want a road in a particular place. In some cases, state revenues can be expected to benefit from the attraction of new businesses and industries and increased tourist traffic.

A major problem for many states is that their highway laws are inadequate to cope with the size and range of problems posed by the advanced design of the new roads.

For example, a survey by the Road Builders shows that although forty-seven of the states have some legal authority to limit access to highways, few of them have what the experts consider adequate authority to carry out the strict access control the new highway law requires.

Acquisition of right of way is going to be troublesome, too. Adequate rights of way at a reasonable price can best be assured by purchase long in advance of construction; attempts to acquire rights of way just before construction are usually more costly and frequently result in delays that throw schedules out of kilter. Yet few states have programs for advance right-of-way purchase. One survey showed that only five states have revolving funds for this purpose. In these states, the highway department purchases rights of way it knows it will someday need with money from the revolving funds. Then when specific projects are authorized and the legislature appropriates the money, the funds spent earlier on land acquisition are paid back into the revolving fund. California officials say their revolving fund has permitted them to buy in advance for $19 million rights of way which would have cost about $114 million if bought just before construction.

Recognizing the shortcomings of state laws on access control and purchase of rights of ways, Congress has written into the new highway law methods by which the Federal Government can lend a hand.

Cities

Many experts see the new highway program as a life-giving transfusion to cities. They believe that if the cities act promptly they can make the new throughways an important part of urban renewal programs, attacking blighted areas, traffic congestion and the general decline of downtown sections with one well financed blow.

Although situations will differ from town to town, the new throughways can, in some cases, help bring about slum clearance projects. They could also prove a blessing to downtown merchants. The throughways will often make it possible for suburbanites to come into the center of town in only a fraction of the time now required and with none of the stop-and-go driving now associated with such a trip. If the downtown parking problem can be licked, and many cities are making progress on that, the throughways and their accompanying belt, loop and feeder roads may revitalize downtown shopping, eating, hotel and entertainment areas in such cities.

City sections of the Interstate System are likely to be the most seriously harassed by land acquisition problems. Many of the urban highway sections will require extremely valuable, highly developed sites and their acquisition will be long and expensive. As a result, it probably will be well into the 1960's before many of the urban sections of the system are built. On the other hand, a few major sections of this type—expressways for New York City and St. Louis are examples—have been in the works a long time and may be among the early projects authorized under the new program.

The Nation

To the motorist, the Interstate System will be a dream come true; to the Federal Government it will mean the correction of an Achilles heel in our defense. Soon after World War II, military leaders decided that the system, linking every productive corner of the country with heavy-duty highways, is as vital a part of our arsenal as are weapons and planes.

The destructive power of atomic and hydrogen bombs make top-grade roads imperative, first, to permit dispersal of industry as a defense measure, and, second, to permit the evacuation of our cities and the swift movement of heavy military equipment if war should come.

BIBLIOGRAPHY

An asterisk (*) preceding a reference indicates that the article or a part of it has been reprinted in this book.

BOOKS, PAMPHLETS, AND DOCUMENTS

Air Transport Association of America. Air transport facts and figures. 17th ed. 23p. The Association. 1107 16th St. Washington 6, D.C. '56.

American Association of Nurserymen. Deadly motoring or planted safety? 12p. The Association. Southern Building. Washington 5, D.C. '56.

American Association of State Highway Officials. History and accomplishment of twenty-five years of federal-aid for highways. 31p. The Association. National Press Building. Washington 4, D.C. '44.

American Association of State Highway Officials. Policy on geometric design of rural highways. 656p. The Association. National Press Building. Washington 4, D.C. '54.

American Association of State Highway Officials. Report on toll roads and their relation to Federal aid. 5p. The Association. National Press Building. Washington 4, D.C. '52.

American Association of State Highway Officials. Road user benefit analyses for highway improvements. 137p. The Association. National Press Building. Washington 4, D.C. '52.

American Association of State Highway Officials. Standard specifications for highway bridges. 328p. The Association. National Press Building. Washington 4, D.C. '53.

American Association of State Highway Officials. Standard specifications for highway materials and methods of sampling and testing. 2v. The Association. National Press Building. Washington 4, D.C. '55.

American Association of State Highway Officials. United States numbered highways. 201p. The Association. National Press Building. Washington 4, D.C. '55.

American Automobile Association. Motor vehicle speed . . . its control and regulation. 9p. The Association. 1712 G St. Washington 6, D.C. '55.

American Automobile Association. Roadside protection. 132p. The Association. 1712 G St. Washington 6, D.C. '51.

American Automobile Association. Sportsmanlike driving. 480p. The Association. 1712 G St. Washington 6, D.C. '55.

American Municipal Association. No outlet: what the lack of a national highway program means to American cities. 24p. The Association. 1625 H St. Washington 6, D.C. '55.

American Petroleum Industries Committee. Toll road facts. 4th ed. 128p. The Committee. 50 W. 50th St. New York 20. '55.

American Trucking Associations. Common sense in highway taxation . . . the case for reciprocity. 41p. The Associations. 1424 16th St. Washington 6, D.C. '54.

Association of American Railroads. Highways: development, use, financing. 158p. The Association. Transportation Building. Washington 6, D.C. '55.

Association of American Railroads. Use and financing of highways; editorial comment. 22p. The Association. Transportation Building. Washington 6, D.C. '56.

Association of American Railroads. Why the gasoline tax—by itself—falls far short of being an equitable way to pay for use of the highways. 4p. The Association. Transportation Building. Washington 6, D.C. '55.

Automobile Manufacturers Association. Automobile facts and figures. 35th ed. 80p. The Association. New Center Building. Detroit 2, Mich. '55.

Automobile Manufacturers Association. What it takes to make your car. 48p. The Association. New Center Building. Detroit 2, Mich. '56.

Automotive Safety Foundation. Parking—how it is financed (prepared for National Retail Dry Goods Association). 48p. The Foundation. Ring Building. Washington 6, D.C. '52.

Automotive Safety Foundation. Safer highway travel for North Dakota (prepared for North Dakota legislative committee). 55p. The Foundation. Ring Building. Washington 6, D.C. '54.

Beggs, A. K. Railway-highway grade crossing problem; economic principles. 55p. Stanford Research Institute. Stanford, Calif. '52.

Behling, B. R. Highway costs . . . and who should pay them; statement before the Committee on Ways and Means, House of Representatives, on H.R. 9075, February 20, 1956. 46p. Association of American Railroads. Transportation Building. Washington 6, D.C. '56.

Bigham, T. C. and Roberts, M. J. Transportation; principles and problems. 710p. McGraw-Hill Book Co. New York. '52.

Billings, Henry. Construction ahead. 158p. Viking Press. New York. '51.

Bradley, Albert. Let's balance the highway ledger; address to the Fifth Highway Transportation Congress, Washington, D.C. May 5, 1954. 15p. National Highway Users Conference. National Press Building. Washington 4, D.C. '54.

Bresnahan, W. A. Tax equity in the federal highway program; statement before the Ways and Means Committee, House of Representatives, February 15, 1956. 15p. American Trucking Associations. 1424 16th St. Washington 6, D.C. '56

Brody, Leon and Stack, H. J. eds. Highway safety and driver education. 464p. Prentice-Hall. New York. '54.

California. Department of Public Works. Division of Highways. Planning Department. Annotated bibliography of planning library references to toll roads and related material. 262p. The Department. Sacramento. '50.

Carey, W. F. Good roads and railroads. 20p. American Trucking Associations. 1424 16th St. Washington 6, D.C. '53.

Chamber of Commerce of the United States. Better roads for our growing nation; report on national conference on highway financing. 56p. The Chamber. Washington 6, D.C. '55.

Chamber of Commerce of the United States. Do bypasses hurt business? 16p. The Chamber. Washington 6, D.C. '50.

Chamber of Commerce of the United States. How bypasses affect business. 24p. The Chamber. Washington 6, D.C. '56.

Chamber of Commerce of the United States. Construction and Civic Development Department. Highway construction, federal-state relations. 11p. The Chamber. Washington 6, D.C. '53.

Chamber of Commerce of the United States. Transportation and Communication Department. Summary Kansas statewide better roads-better business conference, Topeka, September 30, 1954. 16p. The Chamber. Washington 6, D.C. '54.

Chamber of Commerce of the United States. Transportation and Communication Department. Summary Virginia statewide better roads conference, Richmond, December 7, 1954. 21p. The Chamber. Washington 6, D.C. '54.

Chamber of Commerce of the United States. Transportation and Communication Department. Transportation in America. (Information bulletin no28) 9p. The Chamber. Washington 6, D.C. '54.

Chase Manhattan Bank. America's road problem. 23p. The Bank. 18 Pine St. New York 15. '55.

Committee for Economic Development. Modernizing the nation's highways. 25p. The Committee. 444 Madison Ave. New York 22. '56.

Cope, James. Wasted: $3 billions yearly—we can't afford it; statement before the Subcommittee on Roads of the House Committee on Public Works, June 30, 1953. 20p. Automobile Manufacturers Association. New Center Building. Detroit 2, Mich. '53.

Council of State Chambers of Commerce. What federal role in highway construction? (Federal spending facts bulletin no 131) 8p. The Council. 1025 Connecticut Ave. Washington 6, D.C. '55.

Davis, H. E. Issues involved in toll road financing. 14p. Institute of Transportation and Traffic Engineering. University of California. Berkeley. '51.

Davis, H. E. and others. Toll-road developments and their significance in the provision of expressways. (Research Report no 11) 127p. Institute of Transportation and Traffic Engineering. University of California. Berkeley. '53.

Dearing, C. L. American highway policy. 286p. Brookings Institution. Washington, D.C. '41.

Dearing, C. L. and Owen, Wilfred. National transportation policy. 459p. Brookings Institution. Washington, D.C. '49.

Dearing, C. L. and Owen, Wilfred. Toll roads and the problem of highway modernization. 204p. Brookings Institution. Washington, D.C. '51.

English, M. W. and Elmore, J. W. Sales and use taxes and similar taxes affecting motor vehicles. 53p. National Highway Users Conference. National Press Building. Washington 4, D.C. '54.

Fair, M. L. and Williams, E. W. Economics of transportation. 757p. Harper & Bros. New York. '50.

Fisher, H. K. Stretching highway dollars with rubber roads. 52p. Natural Rubber Bureau. 1631 K St. Washington 6, D.C. '52.

Fisher, Yule. Weighed—and found wanting. The experience of ten states which have tried and rejected the ton-mile tax. 11p. National Highway Users Conference. National Press Building. Washington 4, D.C. '54.

Funkhouser, Richard. System approach to rail-truck transport. 19p. Stanford Research Institute. Stanford, Calif. '54.

Geddes, Norman Bel. Magic motorways. 297p. Random House. New York. '40.

General Motors Corporation. How to plan and pay for better highways. 99p. The Corporation. 3044 W. Grand Blvd. Detroit 2, Mich. '53.
Winning entries in Better Highway Awards contest. Robert Moses and others.

Gregory, J. W. Story of the road, from the beginning to A.D. 1931. 311p. G. Maclehose and Company. London. '31.

Hart, Virginia. Story of American roads. 243p. William Sloane Associates. New York. '50.

Hartmann, C. H. Story of the roads. 194p. G. Routledge and Sons. London. '27.

Hebden, Norman and Smith, W. B. State-city relationships in highway affairs. 230p. Yale University Press. New Haven, Conn. '50.

Highway Research Board. Better laws for better highways. (Bulletin 88. Publication 316) 22p. The Board. 2101 Constitution Ave. Washington 25, D.C. '54.

Highway Research Board. Highway finance. (Bulletin 12) 64p. The Board. 2101 Constitution Ave. Washington 25, D.C. '48.

Highway Research Board. Highway finance: selected references, 1950-53. (Bibliography 16. Publication 315) 65p. The Board. 2101 Constitution Ave. Washington 25, D.C. '54.

Highway Research Board. Highway organization and administration. (Bulletin 3) 23p. The Board. 2101 Constitution Ave. Washington 25, D.C. '47.

Highway Research Board. Highway planning and urban development. (Bulletin 64. Publication 249) 12p. The Board. 2101 Constitution Ave. Washington 25, D.C. '52.

Highway Research Board. Highway research organizations: description of existing organizational patterns and scope of activities. (Special Report 15. Publication 284) 44p. The Board. 2101 Constitution Ave. Washington 25, D.C. '53.

Highway Research Board. Highway research review no4. 184p. The Board. 2101 Constitution Ave. Washington 25, D.C. '55.

Highway Research Board. Highway-user taxation. (Bulletin 92. Publication 340) 48p. The Board. 2101 Constitution Ave. Washington 25, D.C. '54.

Highway Research Board. Intergovernmental cooperation in highway affairs. (Special Report 9. Publication 267) 7p. The Board. 2101 Constitution Ave. Washington 25, D.C. '53.

Highway Research Board. Intergovernmental relationships in highway affairs. (Bulletin 66. Publication 255) 15p. The Board. 2101 Constitution Ave. Washington 25, D.C. '53.

Highway Research Board. Know your highway costs. (Special Report 13. Publication 278) 30p. The Board. 2101 Constitution Ave. Washington 25, D.C. '53.

Highway Research Board. Land acquisition. (Bulletin 113. Publication 366) 84p. The Board. 2101 Constitution Ave. Washington 25, D.C. '56.

Highway Research Board. Relocation of public utilities due to highway improvement: an analysis of legal aspects. (Special Report 21. Publication 353) 204p. The Board. 2101 Constitution Ave. Washington 25, D.C. '55.

Highway Research Board. Roadsides: their use and protection. (Special Report 17. Publication 290) 48p. The Board. 2101 Constitution Ave. Washington 25, D.C. '54.

Highway Research Board. Some economic effects of highway improvements. (Bulletin 67. Publication 256) 21p. The Board. 2101 Constitution Ave. Washington 25, D.C. '53.

Highway Research Board. Trends in land acquisition. (Bulletin 101. Publication 349) 82p. The Board. 2101 Constitution Ave. Washington 25, D.C. '55.

Holberg, O. G. Exploring the small community. 199p. University of Nebraska Press. Lincoln 8. '55.

International Road Federation. World road statistics. 122p. The Federation. Washington Bldg. Washington 5, D.C. '53.

Jorgensen, R. E. Priorities and the development of annual highway programs. 31p. National Highway Users Conference. National Press Building. Washington 4, D.C. '52.

Kauer, T. J. Ohio turnpike report. 150p. Ohio State University Press. Columbus. '56.

Kerstetter, J. R. Local governments' share of state collected highway funds and revenue—a 1955 resurvey. 56p. American Municipal Association. 1625 H St. Washington 6, D.C. '55.

*Laas, William, ed. Freedom of the American road. 120p. Ford Motor Company. 3000 Schaefer Road. Dearborn, Michigan. '56.
    Reprinted in this book: Introduction: the American road. Bernard DeVoto. p7-9; How California got fine roads. Samuel W. Taylor. p 10-14; Highways in national defense. Jay Dugan. p 18.

Labatut, Jean and Lane, W. J. eds. Highways in our national life; symposium. 506p. Princeton University Press. Princeton, N.J. '50.

Landon, C. E. Transportation; principles, practices, problems. 618p. William Sloane Associates. New York. '51.

Lawrence, J. V. and Bresnahan, W. A. Trucking industry's position on the national highway program; testimony before the Committee on Public Works, House of Representatives, May 12, 1955. 25p. American Trucking Associations. 1424 16th St. Washington 6, D.C. '55.

League of Kansas Municipalities. Adequate highways and motor vehicle parking. (Special Research Publication no225) 15p. The League. Capitol Federal Building. Topeka. '54.

Lee, A. R. Design of bituminous road compositions. (Rubber in Road Engineering, Technical Note no2) 12p. British Rubber Development Board. Market Buildings, Mark Lane, London, E.C., 3. '54.

Lindholm, R. W. Taxation of the trucking industry. 141p. Bureau of Business Research. Ohio State University. Columbus. '51.

Locklin, D. P. Economics of transportation. 788p. Richard D. Irwin. Chicago. '49.

Mackie, D. I. Highway freighter problem. 72p. Association of American Railroads. Transportation Building. Washington 6, D.C. '50.

Marx, Herbert L. Jr. Community planning. (Reference Shelf. v28, no4) 207p. H. W. Wilson Co. New York. '56.

Maxwell, J. A. Federal grants and the business cycle. 122p. National Bureau of Economic Research. 261 Madison Avenue. New York 16. '52.

Maxwell, J. A. Fiscal impact of federalism in the United States. 427p. Harvard University Press. Cambridge, Mass. '46.

Merrill Lynch, Pierce, Fenner & Beane. Roads and investors. 40p. Merrill Lynch, Pierce, Fenner & Beane. 70 Pine St. New York 5. '55.

Moyer, R. A. Trends and feasibility of toll roads. 12p. Institute of Transportation and Traffic Engineering. University of California. Berkeley. '54.

Mumford, Lewis. Culture of cities. 586p. Harcourt, Brace & Co. New York. '38.

National Association of Motor Bus Operators. Highway tax costs and the motor bus. 12p. The Association. 839 17th St. Washington 6, D.C. '33.

National Grange. Along these roads. 16p. (Published jointly with National Highway Users Conference) The Grange. 744 Jackson Pl. Washington 6, D.C. '53.

National Highway Users Conference. Acceleration of road improvements through bond issues. 17p. The Conference. National Press Building. Washington 4, D.C. '55.

National Highway Users Conference. Digest of federal-aid highway and highway revenue acts of 1956; public law 627. (Information Service Bulletin, July 2, 1956) 8p. The Conference. National Press Building. Washington 4, D.C. '56.

National Highway Users Conference. Digest of policies recommended by the National Highway Users Conference. 8p. The Conference. National Press Building. Washington 4, D.C. '53.

National Highway Users Conference. Diversion, an enemy of good roads. 26p. The Conference. National Press Building. Washington 4, D.C. '52.

National Highway Users Conference. Duplicate taxation. 19p. The Conference. National Press Building. Washington 4, D.C. '54.

National Highway Users Conference. Federal-aid for highways: what it is, how it works. 24p. The Conference. National Press Building. Washington 4, D.C. '56.

National Highway Users Conference. Highway transportation story . . . in facts. 30p. The Conference. National Press Building. Washington 4, D.C. '54.

National Highway Users Conference. Right word. 18p. The Conference. National Press Building. Washington 4, D.C. '55.

National Highway Users Conference. State constitutional limitations on borrowing. 4p. The Conference. National Press Building. Washington 4, D.C. '54.

National Highway Users Conference. Use of federal-aid funds in bond retirement. 4p. The Conference. National Press Building. Washington 4, D.C. '54.

National Municipal League. Model state and regional planning law. 66p. The League. 47 E. 68th St. New York 21. '55.

New York State. Department of Commerce. Local planning and zoning. 83p. The Department. Albany. '53.

Ohio. Department of Highways. Twelfth short course on roadside development. 128p. The Department. Columbus. '53.

Ohio. Department of Highways. Thirteenth short course on roadside development. 114p. The Department. Columbus. '54.

Ohio. Department of Highways. Fourteenth short course on roadside development. 144p. The Department. Columbus. '55.

Owen, Wilfred and Dearing, C. L. Toll roads and the problem of highway modernization. 204p. Brookings Institution. Washington, D.C. '51.

      Adaptation. Traffic Quarterly. 6:141-57. Ap. '52. Why toll roads?

Post, Emily. Motor manners. 46p. National Highway Users Conference. National Press Building. Washington 4, D.C. '49.

Preston, J. A. Federal policy on toll roads. 4p. National Highway Users Conference. National Press Building. Washington 4, D.C. '54.

*Reck, F. M. Car-traveling people. 48p. Automobile Manufacturers Association. New Center Building. Detroit 2, Mich. '55.

Reck, F. M. Horses to horsepower. 48p. Automobile Manufacturers Association. New Center Building. Detroit 2, Mich. '55.

Rose, A. C. Public roads of the past: historic American highways. 183p. American Association of State Highway Officials. National Press Building. Washington 4, D.C. '53.

Rose, A. C. Public roads of the past: 3500 B.C. to 1800 A.D. 101p. American Association of State Highway Officials. National Press Building. Washington 4, D.C. '52.

Roush, C. J. Trucks in 1975. 11p. American Trucking Associations. 1424 16th St. Washington 6, D.C. '53.

Taft, C. A. Commercial motor transportation. 673p. Richard D. Irwin. Chicago. '55.

Thomas, Lowell. New York Thruway story. 48p. Henry Stewart. Buffalo, N.Y. '55.

Tucker, Harry and Leager, J. C. Highway economics. 454p. International Textbook Co. Scranton, Pa. '42.

United States. Commission on Intergovernmental Relations. Report to the President for transmittal to the Congress. 311p. Supt. of Docs. Washington 25, D.C. '55.

United States. Congress. Laws relating to federal-aid in construction of roads 1912-1953. 184p. Supt. of Docs. Washington 25, D.C. '53.

United States. Congress. Needs of the highway systems, 1955-84. (H. Doc. no 120) 22p. 84th Congress, 1st session. Supt. of Docs. Washington 25, D.C. '55.

United States. Congress. Progress and feasibility of toll roads and their relation to the federal-aid program. (H. Doc. no 139) 28p. 84th Congress, 1st session. Supt. of Docs. Washington 25, D.C. '55.

United States. Congress. Report to the President from the President's Advisory Committee on a National Highway Program (Clay Committee). (H. Doc. no93) 27p. 84th Congress, 1st session. Supt. of Docs. Washington 25, D.C. '55.

United States. Department of Commerce. Bureau of Public Roads. Factual discussion of motortruck operation, regulation, and taxation. 113p. Supt. of Docs. Washington 25, D.C. '51.

*United States. Department of Commerce. Bureau of Public Roads. Highways in the United States. 22p. Supt. of Docs. Washington 25, D.C. '54.
> *Reprinted in this book:* Our highway history. p 1-4; Our system of highways. p5-7; Paying for our highways. p8-12.

United States. Department of Commerce. Bureau of Public Roads. Organize your community for traffic safety; reports and recommendations of the White House Conference on Highway Safety, Washington, D.C. February 17-19, 1954. 35p. Supt. of Docs. Washington 25, D.C. '54.

Wager, P. W. ed. County government across the nation. 817p. University of North Carolina Press. Chapel Hill. '50.

PERIODICALS

America. 93:226. Mr. 28, '55. Gore highway bill.

American City. 70:161+. N. '55. Status of highway lighting. E. C. Powers.

American City. 71:155-6. F. '56. Will twenty times more light reduce accidents enough?

American City. 71:169+. Mr. '56. Electronics in highway work. H. A. Radzikowski.

American City. 71:130-2. S. '56. Planning challenge of the federal highway program. B. M. Hayden.

American Home. 55:46+. Ap. '56. Roll your own. Beverly Travers.

American Magazine. 161:24-5+. F. '56. By piggyback across America. E. M. Wylie.

*American Mercury. 73:112-18. N. '51. In defense of trucks. J. S. Worley.

American Mercury. 79:75-7. Ag. '54. Legal highway robbery. V. R. Batdorff.

American Petroleum Institute Proceedings. 34(2):48-53. '54. Your stake in a commonsense highway program. L. F. Thanhouser.

Automotive Industries. 114:1-570. Mr. 15, '56. Thirty-eighth annual statistical issue [entire issue]. J. R. Custer, ed.

Automotive Industries. 115:49-112. D. 1, '56. New America that's coming; analysis of the impact of interstate highway system [entire issue on highways]. J. R. Custer, ed.

Bankers Monthly. 72:21. S. '55. America's road problem; Chase Manhattan bank study of highway financing methods.

Barron's. 32:15-16. Je. 23, '52. Toll roads: turnpike successes reflect motorists' willingness to pay for driver comfort. J. S. Bowen.

Barron's. 36:15-16. Ag. 27, '56. Highways and byways; firms of all kinds will profit from the roadbuilding program. E. M. Haller.

Better Homes and Gardens. 34:68-9+. Ja. '56. More super-roads coming! E. D. Fales, Jr.

Better Homes and Gardens. 34:158. Mr. '56. Safe driving. Wilbur Cross 3d.

Business Week. p 108-10+. Ap. 21, '51. Wrecks cool enthusiasm for toll roads.

Business Week. p42. S. 6, '52. Turnpike business is different; Howard Johnson restaurants.

Business Week. p82-90. S. 13, '52. Crowded free roads result in jumbled network of toll roads.

*Business Week. p70+. N. 22, '52. Where do trucks go from here?

*Business Week. p 106-8. Mr. 7, '53. Nailing down the facts in the truck issue.

*Business Week. p 186-8+. My. 14, '55. New England highway upsets old way of life.

Business Week. p68. Jl. 23, '55. Turndown of N.Y. thruway bid places market in stalemate.

Business Week. p 170. D. 17, '55. More turnpike woes: truckers shun Ohio's tolls, and license row spreads.

Business Week. p 129. F. 4, '56. New fight on auto insurance.

*Business Week. 43-4+. F. 11, '56. Toll roads: is it the end of the boom?

Business Week. p 144. F. 18, '56. Pay-as-you-build highway plan falls short of the revenue mark.

Business Week. p31. Je. 2, '56. Biggest public works in history.

*Business Week. p 166+. Je. 9, '56. Bumpy going for the turnpikes.

*Business Week. p29-30. Je. 30, '56. New roads: thirteen-year look ahead.

Business Week. p72-4+. Ag. 18, '56. They're quickest on the draw in the highway-building program; Texas leads the 48 states but others aren't far behind.

Business Week. p 169. O. 13, '56. I R S gives the bad news on taxes to the nation's heavy truckers.

Changing Times. 7:28-30. Jl. '53. Good and the bad about toll roads.

Christian Century. 72:132-3. F. 2, '55. Roads or schools? an American test.

Civil Engineering. 21:22-4. Ag. '51. Turnpikes are economically justified. E. R. Needles.

Civil Engineering. 23:738-41. N. '53. Highway use determines economic feasibility; New York state thruway. E. B. Isaak.

Civil Engineering. 25:566-9. S. '55. Toll roads; their place in the expanded highway program. T. J. Cambern.

Civil Engineering. 26:1-4+. Ja. '56. Results of Washo road test. W. N. Carey, Jr.

Collier's. 135:102. Je. 24, '55. Life lines and deathtraps.

*Collier's. 137:44-51. Ja. 6, '56. Where are those new roads? T. H. White.

Collier's. 137:80-1. My. 25, '56. Boston's $50,000,000 mile. Leonard Gross.

*Collier's. 138:94. S. 14, '56. Those crazy, mixed-up traffic laws.

Commercial & Financial Chronicle. 181:2305+. My. 19, '55. Developments in municipal finance; toll revenue bonds. C. C. Hardwick.

Commercial & Financial Chronicle. 181:2760+. Je. 16, '55. Toll road legislation and trust indentures. R. L. Mitchell.

Commercial & Financial Chronicle. 183:2826+. Je. 14, '56. Investment banker looks at toll roads. W. H. Steel.

Commercial & Financial Chronicle. 184:777+. Ag. 23, '56. Federal highway program and its implications. E. E. Cook.

Commercial Car Journal. 81:52-3+. Mr. '51. New Jersey turnpike; milestone in highway construction. Bart Rawson.

Commercial Car Journal. 83:51+. Ag. '52. Can we afford Model T roads? H. K. Evans.

Commercial Car Journal. 87:71-8. My. '54. Trucks and the roads they use.

Congressional Digest. 34:131-60. My. '55. President's highway program; background material and pro and con discussion.

Congressional Digest. 35:162. Je. '56. Month in Congress; highway legislation.

Constructor. 34:102-7. Jl. '52. Toll financing—gateway to increasing highway construction.

Consumer Reports. 21:203-5. Ap. '56. Why do auto accidents happen?

Coronet. 32:40-4. Ag. '52. American motorist: number one tax sucker. J. L. Springer.

Coronet. 33:34-7. Ap. '53. Watch that turnpike. J. J. Dugan.

*Coronet. 34:42-6. Je. '53. Tired of paying highway tolls? J. L. Springer.

Coronet. 40:67-71. O. '56. Traffic traps; legal rackets on our roads. Peter Wyden.

*Editorial Research Reports. 1, no 12:225-36. Mr. 23, '54. Automobile liability insurance. H. B. Shaffer.

Editorial Research Reports. 2, no23:887-904. D. 13, '54. New highways. Martin Packman.

Engineer. 200:320-3, 363-6, 400-3. S. 2-16, '55. America's approach to the road problem. W. H. Glanville and R. L. Moore.

Engineering Economist (Stevens Institute of Technology). p2-13. Fall '55. Economics of alternative highway programs. J. P. Buckley.

Engineering News-Record. 147:30-3. O. 18, '51. Are toll highways accident breeders? V. T. Boughton.

Engineering News-Record. 148:21-6. Je. 19, '52. Toll highways become big business. V. T. Boughton.

Engineering News-Record. 157:23-6. Jl. 5, '56. Congress approves bill for $33 billion roads but can the states meet the challenge?

Farm Journal. 79:32-3+. Ag. '55. What to do when the highway comes through. C. W. Gifford.

Farm Journal. 79:166. D. '55. No federal magic, please!

Fortune. 41:102-6. My. '50. Gentle truckers.

Fortune. 47:137-9+. Je. '53. Railroad-trucker brawl.

Fortune. 51:116-20+. My. '55. Those expensive highways. D. A. Saunders.

Fortune. 52:85. S. '55. Those high-priced highways.

Good Housekeeping. 140:26+. Je. '55. Motoring aids imported from Europe. Charlotte Montgomery.

Harper's Magazine. 205:86-91. O. '52. Who shall pay for our roads?
Same abridged. Reader's Digest. 61:41-3. D. '52.

*Harper's Magazine. 213:27-31. D. '56. New super-highways: blessing or blight? Robert Moses.

House & Home. 10:44. Ag. '56. How the $33 billion federal highway program will affect home building.

Investor's Reader. 18:1-40. Je. 4, '52. American roads [entire issue]. Alma deCoen, ed.

Iron Age. 178:52. Ag. 2, '56. Highways; what big program requires.

Life. 38:104-6+. My. 30, '55. Dead end for the U.S. highway. Herbert Brean.

*Look. 17:76+. Je. 16, '53. Tax road or toll road? George Koether.

*Look. 19:65-9. S. 6, '55. Are we buying another traffic jam? George Koether.

Look. 20:84+. My. 15, '56. Case of the care-less car. George Koether.

Magazine of Wall Street. 93:658-60+. Mr. 6, '54. How we have outgrown our new transportation arteries. W. L. Radford.

Midwest Engineer. 3:10-13+. My. '51. Solution to highway problems, tollways. C. E. DeLeuw.

NACA (National Association of Cost Accountants) Bulletin. 33:1315-27. Jl. '52. Accounting system of the New Jersey turnpike. H. A. Wegener.

*Nation. 182:357-60. Ap. 28, '56. Our strangling highways. David Cort.

Nation. 183:175-78. S. 1, '56. Death on Labor Day. David Cort.

National Geographic Magazine. 110:567-618. N. '56. New York state's new Main Street; Thruway. M. C. McDade.

National Municipal Review. 44:56-8. Mr. '55. Clay committee submits huge highway program.

National Petroleum News. 44:38-9. Je. 11, '52. Toll roads can work fine if traffic count is high.

National Tax Journal. 5:97-106. Je. '52. The pricing of highway services. J. M. Buchanan.

National Underwriter. 60:15. Ag. 23, '56. More states adopt Road Aid plan.

Nation's Business. 39:68-9. F. '51. Acorns of industry; from pikes to highways. R. W. Howard.

Nation's Business. 39:50-5. My. '51. For whom the toll roads. Magruder Dobie.

Nation's Business. 40:34-7+. D. '52. Roads we could have bought. Booton Herndon.

Nation's Business. 41:30-1+. Ap. '53. Road blocks to good highways. W. J. Slocum.

Nation's Business. 41:30-3+. Jl. '53. Divided authority blocks better roads. Booton Herndon.

Nation's Business. 42:50+. Mr. '54. Toll road boom; 10,000 miles for $10,000,000,000. H. K. Evans.

Nation's Business. 42:77-81. N. '54. Their roads pay for themselves. H. K. Evans.

Nation's Business. 43:58-62. F. '55. Here's the President's highway plan. H. K. Evans.

Nation's Business. 43:38-40. S. '55. Highway radar is watching you.

Nation's Business. 43:41+. S. '55. Engineers' traffic tricks save lives.

Nation's Business. 44:36-7+. F. '56. Traffic jam costs $25,000,000,000. Robinson Newcomb.

*Nation's Business. 44:32-3+. Ap. '56. Slow traffic laws waste fast roads. J. E. Johnston.

*Nation's Business. 44:32-3+. Jl. '56. New roads: changed business pattern ahead. C. B. Seib.

*Nation's Business. 44:96-7+. S. '56. Your state may block new roads. P. B. Yeager.

Nation's Business. 44:103-5. S. '56. Here's way to end city traffic jam. Wilfred Owen.

Nature Magazine. 48:369. Ag. '55. Which do you prefer?

New York Herald Tribune. sec9, p2. O. 5, '52. Highway problem; vast construction program is urged; U.S. figures total cost at nearly $50 billion; toll pike emerges as one solution; truckers see double taxation.

New York Herald Tribune. sec9, p2. O. 5, '52. State toll road boom creating a superhighway across nation.

New York Journal-American. sec 1, p 1+. F. 1, '52. Hearst road plan for better roads (editor's report). W. R. Hearst, Jr.

New York Times. p3. Mr. 9, '52. The high road or the low road; a driver tests regular routes and turnpikes from here to Ohio. David Landman.

New York Times. p F 1+. Jl. 1, '56. Hard facts on 'pike: it's cheaper to lift tolls than switch bonds. Paul Heffernan.

New York Times. p26. Jl. 22, '56. Secretary [of Commerce] Weeks announces building standards for highways under new federal program.

New York Times. p F 1+. Jl. 29, '56. Detour is ahead in turnpike era. Paul Heffernan.

New York Times. p F 1+. Jl. 29, '56. Traffic directed by electronics. A. R. Zipser.

New York Times. p F 1+. S. 9, '56. Big road program comes to [bond] market. Paul Heffernan.

New York Times. p F 1+. N. 4, '56. Turnpike issues are on seesaw; prices drop but earnings rise. Paul Heffernan.

New York Times. p R 1+. N. 11, '56. Roads raise issue of condemnation. J. P. Callahan.

New York Times Magazine. p 14. S. 5, '54. Super-byway: the country road. Hal Borland.

    Same. Reader's Digest. 66:45-6. Ap. '55.

New York Times Magazine. p26. F. 13, '55. Exit for the motorcycle cop. George Barrett.

*New York Times Magazine. p 15. D. 18, '55. Auto accidents: causes, cures. S. J. Williams.

    Discussion. p67. Ja. 8, '56.

Newsweek. 42:61-2. Ag. 24, '53. Economy building for a nation on wheels.

Newsweek. 44:19-20. Jl. 26, '54. Plan and prejudice.

Newsweek. 44:80. Ag. 2, '54. States and the gas tax. Raymond Moley.

Newsweek. 44:82+. O. 18, '54. Needed 100 billion.

Newsweek. 45:65. Mr. 7, '55. Road issue is money.

Newsweek. 45:112. Mr. 21, '55. Clay highway plan. Raymond Moley.

Newsweek. 45:96. Je. 27, '55. Speed, the killer. Raymond Moley.

Newsweek. 46:33. S. 26, '55. Straightaway; New York to Chicago.

Newsweek. 47:29-30. Mr. 5, '56. Slaughter on our highways.

Newsweek. 47:101-5. My. 14, '56. Jam on the highways.

Oil and Gas Journal. 54:122-5. My. 21, '56. What the highway bill means to oil.

Popular Mechanics. 100:82-8. Jl. '53. Million-dollar-a-mile toll roads. Dick Frederic.

Popular Mechanics. 104:131. S. '55. Portrait of a highway.

Popular Science. 168:140-4+. My. '56. U.S. plans 40,000-mile road to everywhere. G. B. Soule.

Public Roads. 27:57-88. O. '52. Recent trends in highway bond financing. H. C. Duzan and others.

Public Roads. 27:127-53. Ap. '53. Road-user and property taxes on selected motor vehicles, 1953. E. M. Cope and R. W. Meadows.

Public Roads. 28:17-26. Je. '54. Estimate of user taxes paid by vehicles in different type and weight groups. E. M. Cope and others.

Public Roads. 29:37-67. Ag. '56. Road-user and property taxes on selected motor vehicles. E. M. Cope and L. L. Liston.

Reader's Digest. 56:137-40. Je. '50. Rape of our roads. F. G. Brownell.

Reader's Digest. 66:73-4. Mr. '55. Man who didn't look hurt. Allan Keller.

Reader's Digest. 67:105-7. Jl. '55. I'm a tough cop. John Carlson; ed. by A. E. Hotchner.

Reader's Digest. 67:128-30. O. '55. State of Washington vs highway slaughter. Roderic Olzendam.

Reporter. 13:14-23. Ag. 11, '55. Engineering of consent; a case study. Robert Bendiner.

Roads and Streets. 95:70-1. Jl. '52. Gallup poll shows people favor toll super-roads.

Rotarian. 88:26-31. Mr. '56. Modern highways: how to get them; symposium.
    Reply. 88:1. Je. '56.
Rotarian. 88:30. Mr. '56. Master plan must recognize the place of privately financed toll highways. A. J. Wedeking.

Rubber Developments (London). 8:54-60. Summer '55. Progress of rubber in roads. A. R. Smee.

*Saturay Evening Post. 223:19-21+. S. 16, '50. Are trucks destroying our highways? D. G. Wittels.

Saturday Evening Post. 226:42-3+. Mr. 13, '54. World's worst traffic tangle. F. J. Taylor.

Saturday Evening Post. 227:28-9+. F. 5, '55. Case of the obsolete highways. Richard Thruelsen.
    Discussion. 227:4. Mr. 12, '55.
Saturday Evening Post. 227:10. My. 21, '55. Why make our children pay for our highways? F. R. Sproule.

*Saturday Evening Post. 228:17+. O. 22, '55. Let's put sense in the accident laws. S. H. Hofstadter; ed. by J. A. Morris.

Saturday Evening Post. 228:41+. Ja. 28, '56. Traffic is a monster. Rufus Jarman.

Saturday Evening Post. 228:48-9+. My. 5, '56. I drive the turnpikes and survive. P. W. Kearney.

Saturday Evening Post. 228:36+. Je. 30, '56. Swindlers on the turnpikes. J. A. Morris.

Saturday Evening Post. 229:10. S. 8, '56. States also must build more highways.

Saturday Evening Post. 229:31+. S. 8, '56. How we cut our auto death rate. A. A. Ribicoff.

Saturday Evening Post. 229:23+. O. 20, '56. Coast to coast without a stoplight. Richard Thruelsen.

Science Digest. 38:31-5. D. '55. Who should pay for auto accidents? M. E. Knight.

Science Digest. 39:16. Ap. '56. Nature's speed laws.

Science Digest. 39:77-80. My. '56. You can't cheat the turnpike. Glenn Infield.

Science News Letter. 67:120. F. 19, '55. Electronic brain can solve traffic problems; discrete-variable simulator.

Scientific Monthly. 78:380-7. Je. '54. Blueprint for *autobahn* U. S. A. P. F. Griffin.

Senior Scholastic. 68:30-1. F. 16, '56. Horsepower, enemy of horse sense? pro and con discussion.

Senior Scholastic. 68:14-15. My. 3, '56. Breaking the highway program bottleneck.

State Government. 28:79-81+. Ap. '55. For an adequate highway system. L. D. Clay.

Tax Digest. 33:121-2+. Ap. '55. Federal highway aid proposal: violent departures not justified. H. F. Byrd.

Tax Economics Bulletin. 21:1-2. Ja.-F. '56. Traffic deaths: causes and cures.

Time. 64:61. D. 20, '54. Green light for truckers.

Time. 65:78. F. 28, '55. Better highways; private toll roads show the way.

Time. 65:23. Je. 6, '55. Well-botched job.

Time. 67:35-6. Ap. 9, '56. Red light on the turnpike.

Time. 67:36. My. 7, '56. $52 billion face lifting.

Time. 68:98-102. N. 19, '56. Paying the highway toll.

Town Meeting (Bulletin of America's Town Meeting of the Air). 20, no46:1-12. '55. President's highway plan. Francis Case; G. A. Dondero.

Traffic Engineering. 24:233-5. Ap. '54. The car and the road.

Traffic Quarterly. 5:141-7. Ap. '52. Why toll roads? Wilfred Owen and C. L. Dearing.

Traffic Quarterly. 8:76-83. Ja. '54. What does the motorist expect of today's highway system? K. B. Rykken.

Traffic Quarterly. 10:169-80. Ap. '56. Interstate system. A. E. Johnson.

Traffic Quarterly. 10:181-9. Ap. '56. Suburban shopping center effects on highways and parking. Homer Hoyt.

U. S. News & World Report. 29:30-3. D. 29, '50. Future of the highways. T. H. MacDonald.

U. S. News & World Report. 36:74+. Mr. 5, '54. Traffic jams are here to stay.

U. S. News & World Report. 38:64. Mr. 4, '55. Here's Ike's highway plan.

U. S. News & World Report. 38:114+. Ap. 8, '55. Billions for roads, but not enough.

U. S. News & World Report. 38:53-6. My. 27, '55. Where road billions will go.

U. S. News & World Report. 39:52-3. S. 9, '55. What's blocking new roads?

*U. S. News & World Report. 40:50-1. F. 3, '56. Highway deaths are rising.

U. S. News & World Report. 40:134+. F. 10, '56. $51.5 billions for roads?

U. S. News & World Report. 40:33-5. Je. 8, '56. Will 50 billion dollars end traffic jams?

U. S. News & World Report. 40:27-30. Je. 29, '56. Who will get the 50 billions for roads?

U. S. News & World Report. 41:72-80. Jl. 20, '56. No more traffic jams? Interview. C. D. Curtiss.

U. S. News & World Report. 41:68-73. S. 14, '56. City-by-city report: how freeways will break traffic bottlenecks of big cities.

Vital Speeches of the Day. 15:536-7. Je. 15, '49. Highways in the public service. T. H. MacDonald.

Vital Speeches of the Day. 22:298-301. Mr. 1, '56. Motor transport. R. A. Fruehauf.